MW00698573

Who's Afraid of Modern Art?

WHO'S AFRAID of MODERN ART?

Essays on Modern Art & Theology in Conversation

Daniel A. Siedell

Foreword by
Robyn O'Neil

CASCADE *Books* · Eugene, Oregon

WHO'S AFRAID OF MODERN ART?
Essays on Modern Art & Theology in Conversation

Cascade Books
An Imprint of Wipf and Stock Publishers
199 W. 8th Ave., Suite 3
Eugene, OR 97401

www.wipfandstock.com

ISBN 13: 978-1-62564-442-8

Cataloguing-in-Publication Data

Siedell, Daniel A., 1966–

   Who's afraid of modern art? : essays on modern art and theology in conversation / Daniel A. Siedell.

   xviii + 160 p. ; 23 cm. Includes bibliographical references.

   ISBN 13: 978-1-62564-442-8

   1. Painting, Modern—20th century. 2. Painting, Modern—21st century. 3. Art and society—History—20th century. 4. Art and society—History—21st century. I. Title.

BR115.A8 S58 2015

Manufactured in the U.S.A.   01/06/2015

Do not interpretations belong to God?

—GENESIS 40:8

"Asher Lev, [art] is a tradition of goyim and pagans. Its values are goyisch and pagan. Its concepts are goyisch and pagan. Its way of life is goyisch and pagan."

—JACOB KAHN, IN CHAIM POTOK, *MY NAME IS ASHER LEV*

[D]o not venture into the metaphysics of the fine arts without being initiated into the orgies and Eleusinian mysteries.

—J.G. HAMANN

CONTENTS

ILLUSTRATIONS

Cover: Robyn O'Neil, *Red Sky*, 2013; oil pastel & graphite on paper, 8 ½ x 5 ½ inches; Courtesy of Artist and Talley Dunn Gallery, Dallas, Texas.

Frontispiece, Robyn O'Neil, *Come, all that is quiet*, 2009; graphite on paper; 60 x 60 in. Courtesy of the Artist and Talley Dunn Gallery, Dallas, Texas.

Figure 1: Robyn O'Neil, *These final hours embrace at last; this is our ending, this is our past*, 2007; graphite on paper; 83 x 166 ¾ inches; collection of The Modern Art Museum, Fort Worth, Texas. Gift of Marshall R. Young Oil Co. in Honor of George Marshall Young, Sr., Chairman.

Figure 2: Robyn O'Neil, *Hell*, 2008–2011, triptych, graphite on paper; 82 x 172 inches; Courtesy of the Artist and Susan Inglett Gallery, New York.

Back Image, Robyn O'Neil, *These final hours embrace* (detail).

FOREWORD

It is not light that we need, but fire;
it is not the gentle shower, but thunder.
We need the storm, the whirlwind, and the earthquake

—FREDERICK DOUGLASS

Dan Siedell is a rare gift to artists. We aren't typically gifted with feeling understood. In fact, that lack of understanding might be exactly why we make art. Every image, an attempt to find someone who might recognize something familiar, might fathom what we reveal in our work. Reading Dan's essays is akin to finding a secret ally. He fights the war with us. He shines the flashlight into our shadows; sweeps the cave. It is not to be taken lightly, what he does, because most people are not compelled to remain in the wake of an artist's path. It can be, as he so beautifully and often describes, a terrifying endeavor. Yet he does it, again and again, with reverence and with heart. And he's brave enough to love that the very thing he's trying to wrangle is the most perplexing paragon.

Artists often attempt to unearth thoughts that might be easier left dormant and ignored. We excavate, we visually proclaim. Dive in, expose, assess. And after this nonstop process of molding and scrutiny, our work is displayed, made vulnerable to be seen and deciphered. It is then that we yearn for something else, a conversation. We need proof that what we've created might just make sense to someone. And that's when Dan comes in, to illuminate. With language, with bottomless understanding, with a way of crystallizing incredibly mysterious things, some of those things being mysterious even to us, the people who have created them.

It is my radical belief that it takes kindness and compassion to truly get to the center of art, to feel it swimming in your pores. Dan Siedell is

xi

the reason I know this to be true. His unparalleled intellect is met with his empathy, and as a result, we are blessed with words that will go down in history. This book of essays should, and no doubt will, be required reading for a long time to come for artists, art lovers, Christians, the spiritually involved and curious, or even if you're simply human. These essays will make you wonder what should matter, and they'll help you see the unseen. In his essay "Who's Afraid of Modern Art?," Dan notes that caring about modern art is what he's been called to do with his life. He praises God for his being fearful of modern art. To be, as he is, in love with something that causes such grief, confusion, suffering . . . well, one can't get any nobler than that.

Robyn O'Neil

ACKNOWLEDGMENTS

I am thankful that my editor Rodney Clapp took the chance to publish an unusual book like this. Tim Dalrymple at *Patheos* gave me the opportunity to write regularly about art, culture, and theology at a crucial time. Many of the essays included in this book have their origins, in one way or another, as blog posts for *Patheos*.

Robyn O'Neil's drawings have had a significant influence on my work as a critic and curator. Having had the privilege to write about her work on several occasions over the years, I am thus honored that she has graciously agreed to return the favor.

Dr. Jonathan A. Linebaugh, Associate Professor of New Testament at Knox Theological Seminary in Fort Lauderdale, Florida, has been a friend, conversation partner, and theological mentor.

Although they were written in Fort Lauderdale, many of these essays were conceived in Charlottesville, Virginia. During my time as Scholar in Residence at the New City Arts Initiative in Charlottesville, I had the opportunity to think and talk about modern art and theology with numerous conversation partners, and the late Patricia Jones and John McCray were extraordinary hosts. The first essay, "Who's Afraid of Modern Art?" exists only because Paul Walker, Rector of Christ Episcopal Church in Charlottesville, invited me to speak on the subject. Rev. Greg Thompson, Senior Pastor of Trinity Presbyterian Church in Charlottesville, has offered crucial intellectual and pastoral support. David Zahl, Executive Director of Mockingbird Ministries, has been a consistent source of encouragement. My gratitude extends to the entire Mockingbird family, especially William McDavid, who provided rigorous and insightful editorial work on the manuscript. Dr. Michael Horton of the White Horse Inn and Westminster Theological Seminary in Escondido, California has encouraged me in numerous ways, not least of which has been his insatiable curiosity about this strange cultural practice called "modern art."

The final stages of this book benefited immensely from the institutional support of The King's College in New York City, where I was appointed Presidential Scholar and Art Historian in Residence in September 2013. It has created the intellectual space for me to continue to do what I do among supportive and talented faculty, eager and intelligent students, and under the humane leadership of Dr. Harry Bleattler, Chair of the Division of Media, Culture, and the Arts, and President Greg Thornbury, to whom I am grateful for his commitment to the work I do. I also want to thank Rev. Jacob Smith, Dusty Brown, and my friends at Calvary/St. George's Episcopal Church, which has become my church home away from home.

When my family moved from Nebraska to south Florida in July 2011, Pastor Tullian Tchividjian promised us that Coral Ridge Presbyterian Church would become our family in south Florida. We did not realize how true his words would be. Tullian's tireless proclamation of God's mercy and grace, his support for my vocation, and his friendship are, more so than he realizes, responsible not only for this book, but for so much more since that summer of 2011.

My wife, Kerri, and children, Daniel, Morgan, and Jacob, whose lives have been marked in one way or another by my love of modern and contemporary art, have been a constant source of support. They have taught me that there is no greater gift in life than to be loved and to love. It has been this love that has enabled me to freely pursue my love of art.

It is to Kerri, "my sweetest friend" (the Goo Goo Dolls), who stood with me one afternoon in front of Jackson Pollock's magnificent painting *Autumn Rhythm* (1950) at the Metropolitan Museum of Art twenty-five years ago, and continues to stand with me, that I dedicate this book.

"And when we're old and near the end we'll go home and start again" (the Goo Goo Dolls).

INTRODUCTION

An artist I work with invites me to his studio to see some new paintings he is working on for an upcoming show. It marks a new direction, he thinks, but he's not sure if they amount to anything. Other than his wife, I am the first person to whom he has shown them. Standing in the middle of his workroom, I am confronted by six canvases, each in various stages of completion. He asks, "What do you think?"

At this moment, in this situation, standing before particular works of art, most discourse on art falls terribly short. And it is at this moment that Oscar Wilde's surprising declaration, spoken by Gilbert in "The Critic as Artist," rings most true:

> More difficult to do a thing than to talk about it? Not at all. That is a gross popular error. It is very much more difficult to talk about a thing than to do it.[1]

A scrap of canvas with smelly pigments smeared across it is a vulnerable artifact, confronting the viewer through the most immediate of senses. It unfolds an experience only gradually through time. Moreover, this vulnerable artifact, susceptible to the often hasty and impatient judgments of vision, also emerges precariously from language—words, sentences, talk—to which it can too easily and too quickly return. The artist tells me that he read a line in Tolstoy's novella, *The Death of Ivan Illych*, which "created space for some paintings." The canvases that surround me in his workroom are those that Tolstoy's sentence wrought. And yet as visual artifacts they have their own particular existence in the world that cannot be reduced to words, sentences, talk—cannot even be reduced to or confined by that one sentence of Tolstoy's.

And as I experience these unfinished paintings and begin to reflect on the feelings and emotions that their visual appearance generates,

1. Wilde, "The Critic As Artist," 209.

the artist asks for my response—through language, that is; through my own words, sentences, and talk. He is not asking for my art historical interpretation or a philosophical discourse. He is asking for language that is a response to *my* experience of the paintings—what do I see, what do I hear, and thus what are they saying and doing *to me*?

But this is precisely at the moment where language about art usually fails to offer any help. To the contrary, it often seems as if talking about art, both inside and outside the church, is committed to avoiding this moment. Talk about art outside the church swirls around fashion and entertainment, about the perpetual "newness" of political, social, and cultural relevance that "everyone" (always in the abstract) knows or needs to know. And talk about art inside the church gravitates toward the abstract and conceptual, from the timeless and ahistorical vagaries of transcendence and the spiritual to the disembodied abstractions of the good, the true, and the beautiful, or the deceptive abstractions of world view analysis. Both approaches—one obsessed with the ephemerality of fashion and the other preoccupied with the idealism of the transcendent—tend to leave untouched how a particular person is addressed by a particular work of art.

Wilde's surprising claims about the difficulty of talking about art responds to the challenge that the concrete particularity of a painting poses for language. "The highest criticism," Wilde declares, again through Gilbert, "deals with art not as expressive but as impressive purely."[2] Works of art, like the paintings I stand before in this artist's studio, exist to be experienced—to be heard—by a single individual. And it is this impression that is the "work" of the painting, and it is this impression with which the critic, according to Wilde, should ultimately concern herself.

Yet the work of art is not a Rorschach test, an image upon which the viewer or the critic can simply impose his experience, ideas, or feelings. *It* makes the first move. It addresses. It does not merely confirm the viewer's experience, emotion, or feeling, but deepens, changes, or perhaps even contradicts them. It initiates or makes possible a viewer's experience, but that experience, that emotion, that feeling did not—could not—exist prior to the viewer being addressed by that painting.

But what the painting "says" when it addresses me is often a source of confusion and frustration. Too often we consider a work of art to be an "image" that we have to "read" in order to get to the "ideas," "meanings," "world view," or "values" that are buried or hidden amidst its visual features. We imagine that the aesthetic experience of the work is either a "distraction" through which we must sift in order to get to the "meaning" or we presume

2. Ibid.

that its capacity to connect emotionally and through the affections is simply a means to address the intellect through the heart. Like Lewis Carroll's Humpty Dumpty, we presume we can find "meaning" anywhere, even in paint-smeared scraps of canvas. But, as Wilde's Gilbert observes, "the aim of art is simply to create a mood."[3] That this aim strikes us as insignificant and unimportant is an indication of just how unwilling we are to grant significance and importance to our emotional life, to the life of the affections, which our intellectual life informs.

The challenge of talking about a painting, then, is to maintain, through *words*, the integrity of the distinctive aesthetic experience that it can offer *visually*; to use those words and sentences, not to explain, interpret, judge, or otherwise *reduce* but to *expand* the experiential space that allows the painting to address the viewer. This challenge is greater still when the words are not spoken in proximity to the painting, whether in the artist's studio or in a gallery or museum, but when those words are *written* or published and thus achieve a life of their own as cultural artifacts. These words and sentences can do two things simultaneously. First, they can create a compelling experience for the reader *as literature*, as its own aesthetic experience, of which the work of art and the critic that stands before it are the protagonists. And second, these words and sentences can open imaginative space for the reader in anticipation of encountering the work under consideration, or, in fact, *any subsequent work of art* that the reader might encounter in the future. That this book does not contain reproductions of the works of art discussed in these essays is evidence of my commitment to the broader responsibility of talking (and writing) about works of art as a means to encourage and prepare a reader to stand before *any* work of art.

Moreover, "talking about a thing," as Wilde puts it, is an opportunity to curse as well as bless, to destroy as well as give life (Jas 3:10). And so for Wilde, the critic's words is nothing if not life-giving, a "creation within a creation," as he calls it, because "the critic occupies the same relation to the work of art that he criticizes as the artist does to the visible world of form and colour, or the unseen world of passion and thought."[4] But the work of art is not merely a pretense for the expression of the critic's political, cultural, or theological social agenda, or not merely an excuse for the critic to exercise his creative expression. It is the painting that is the impetus, as an artifact that *is there*, existing outside the critic, an artifact that initiates and generates the critic's experience as it addresses the one who stands before it. And it is this relationship between the viewer who stands addressed by a

3. Ibid.
4. Ibid., 199.

scrap of canvas with paint smeared across it that is profoundly theological, that opens a space for that artifact to address the viewer. The church presumes that a work of art's theological importance is determined exclusively by the subject matter of the content of the work of art or the beliefs or intentions of the artist that produced it. And this presumption has had serious consequences for Christian reflection on aesthetic experience.

"My art," Edvard Munch observed, "is self-confession. Through it I seek to clarify my relationship to the world." But Munch also goes further, hoping that his pictures "might be able to help others to clarify their own search for truth."[5] The essays in this book are part of my own search for truth and its implications in and through a cultural practice to which I have devoted more than twenty-five years. They are also my confession of faith in art as well as the God whose Word gives it life and enables it to speak (Col 1).

In the artist's studio I stand before paintings that address me.
How will I respond?

---

5. Quoted in Tøjner, *Munch in His Own Words*, 135.

WHO'S AFRAID OF MODERN ART?[1]

Let's face it. Modern art is strange and off-putting. It doesn't behave like we think art should, not impressing us with the artist's technical capacity to represent a world with which we are familiar and helping us decorate our interior and exterior environments. And so a painting that features distorted, tortured, and emaciated figures, garish colors, and, to our eyes, poorly drawn trees, seems to perform no real artistic function in the world, except to put us on edge. We're confused that some small pastel and oil drawing, *The Scream*, painted in 1895 by Edvard Munch, a neurotic Norwegian, sold for $120 million dollars at Sotheby's in 2011. Or that two years later at Christie's, Francis Bacon's triptych of Lucien Freud sold for over $140 million. What are we missing? How can anyone pay that kind of money for pigments smeared across a piece of paper or a scrap of canvas? In fact, we are hard-pressed to account for why anyone would pay even a few hundred dollars for a painting. And so someone must be pulling our leg.

And yet there is something else that haunts us. Perhaps it's not just a sham, a joke, or a hobby for critical theorists and continental philosophers—perhaps modern art is dangerous. Perhaps it actually teaches us to see the world in ways that produce vice. Perhaps it is a practice that causes us to lose our faith.

Perhaps modern art is something to fear.

1. A version of this essay was originally presented at Christ Episcopal Church, Charlottesville, Virginia, May 1, 2013. Another version was presented at The King's College, New York City, November 19, 2013.

1

My remarks will not ease these fears.

Tonight I come clean about my twenty-five-year relationship with modern art. I will testify to what modern art has done to me as a Christian and as a human being.

In a pivotal scene in *Walk the Line,* the 2005 movie starring Joaquin Phoenix as Johnny Cash, record producer Sam Phillips interrupts Cash's rather bland rendition of a popular gospel song to tell him that he doesn't need his kind of music. Cash is offended, naturally, and asks why. Phillips responds, "because I don't believe you." Cash thinks that Phillips is accusing him of not believing in God. But Phillips's accusation runs deeper. When Cash complains, "you didn't let us bring it home," Phillips loses patience.

> You want to bring it home? Let's bring it home:

> If you was hit by a truck and you were lying in the gutter dying and you had time to sing one song before you turn to dirt, one song that lets others and God know about how you felt about your time on this earth . . . one song that would sum you up, you tell me that you would sing that song, about how you are "filled with joy" and that you're "gonna shout it?" Or would you sing something different . . . something real?

Tonight, I'm going to follow Sam Phillips's advice. I will sing something different, something real about my experience with modern art, something that reflects what I think about my time on this earth.

Tonight I will make a confession.

I've given my life to modern art and to the artists that have painted in its wake. And I have felt the pressure to justify my interest in and passion for modern art *as a Christian*—to step away from my work as an art history professor, museum curator, and art critic to defend my relationship to it theologically and spiritually—even to respond to the accusation that modern art and I have been, as St. Paul warns, "unequally yoked."

I was born and reared on the plains of Nebraska and grew up in a large nondenominational church, both of which, as I look back on it, make my interest in the arts, and modern art in particular, especially perplexing. My father would have described himself at the time (as he still does) as a neo-evangelical after Carl Henry, with his approach to culture shaped by Francis Schaeffer and his imagination formed by a particular evangelical reading of C. S. Lewis's novels and apologetics. My father was addicted to opera, classical music, and history, but our home wasn't a bastion of high culture. I never went to art museums as a child. Our house was not filled with paintings and sculptures or with the people who would collect them.

Nebraskans and evangelicals are skeptical of art—it's not useful enough to justify its existence. It smells of the elitist or the bohemian—of the drawing room or the coffee house. Given the fact that my passion for modern art seemed to have appeared out of nowhere, it suggested to my friends and fellow congregants (including the elders' board that guarded the flock) that I was not someone to be trusted.

One encounter can be taken as paradigmatic. I had recently been appointed Chief Curator of the Sheldon Museum of Art, my hometown university art museum, which has one of the most well-known collections of American art in the country. And in the Sunday arts section an article had appeared announcing my appointment. At church later that morning, during our meet and greet, an elder sitting in front of me turned around, shook my hand, congratulated me on my appointment, and then, looking me in the eye, declared, "Now you can take down all the nudes on display in the museum."

This was not exactly the kind of "greeting" I was expecting, but an accurate indicator of the belief that art is more trouble than it is worth—it is something that has to be cleaned up and taken out, controlled, kept at arm's length; it's certainly not something to be embraced.

All this to say, modern art is neither something I discovered nor something expected, through my nature or nurture. It is something, in retrospect, that I can only say *happened* to me.

My love of modern art didn't even start with a painting. It started with prose.

As an undergraduate at the University of Nebraska I happened upon the essays of a critic working in New York, Donald B. Kuspit, whose writing about the most difficult and enigmatic artists, like Andy Warhol, Jackson Pollock, and Marcel Duchamp, made me feel that I needed to know them and discover the secret of their work.[2]

Let me reiterate: it was not some extraordinary encounter with a masterpiece at the Metropolitan Museum or the Louvre that ignited my passion for art—it was the critic's sentences. And in his reviews and essays, there was not a single reproduction of any of the work he addressed. Simply through Kuspit's seriousness, passion, imagination, and the references and connections that the works of art seemed to extract from him—from Goethe and D. W. Winnicott to Rilke, Marx, Freud, and Sartre—I could sense that Kuspit had to bring his intellectual and emotional A-game to the encounter—and the result was electrifying. Perhaps what fascinated me the most was that a scrap of canvas with oil paint smeared around it could ignite such

2. Kuspit, *The Critic is Artist.*

intellectual passion—it was, I must admit, both intoxicating *and* perplexing. His words were poetry; they sung. But, *I felt them before I could understand them.*

Those sentences that referred to paintings I couldn't even see imputed to them life-giving dignity, while deepening the mystery of the world. I began to feel the importance of human beings that devoted their lives to smearing oil paints on scraps of canvas and human beings that lived to write about them and exhibit and collect their work. Kuspit's words did something else as well. They revealed the mystery of myself to myself. That is, I began to sense that taking art seriously—looking at it, thinking about it, and writing about it—was not so much about interpreting the work of art as it was receiving it, listening to its effect on me. And I then began to experience that strange feeling of detachment—of thinking about myself thinking and feeling myself feeling—that would be an important part of my relationship with modern art and an important part of my development as a human being. To experience a work of art was to allow it first to interpret me.

And so after graduation I left Nebraska for New York City to study with that critic. For two years I ate, slept, and drank modern art. I looked at classical Greek statuary, Renaissance paintings, and Velázquez's portraits at the Met, medieval manuscripts at the Morgan Library, and the Vermeers at the Frick. But it was modern art—the hard stuff—at MoMA, the Whitney, the Guggenheim, and the galleries in SoHo, which seduced me.

The damage had been done.

I returned to the Midwest to get married and to do my doctoral work, which, incidentally, focused on the artists and critics of the New York art world in the 1940s and 1950s. And although I returned to Nebraska to begin my career as a curator and art historian, I have never recovered from what modern art did to me those two years in New York.

I grew up in a conservative evangelical Christian home and I cannot remember a time when I didn't consider myself a Christian. I did not go through a period of rejecting the church or rejecting my faith. And it never dawned on me that my work with modern art needed to be "reconciled" with my faith, or that I needed a "Christian world view" in order to negotiate the minefield of modern art or the art world. I loved Jesus. And I loved looking at and thinking about Jackson Pollock's drip paintings. My love of modern art seemed as natural as my faith in Christ. That of course didn't mean that there were no tensions, but I never considered that I needed a systematic theological framework to justify my interest in modern art.

However, as I began to pursue theological and historical questions related to my own church tradition, my lack of a systematic theological framework for art began to bother me. I wished I'd thought theologically about my work before I attended graduate school, had a Christian world view screwed on tight, perhaps from a Christian college education, which could have equipped me to think about how I could integrate my faith and work.

But the burden to justify myself theologically was inevitable. It began when I was putting the finishing touches on my doctoral dissertation on the critics of Abstract Expressionism. I picked up Francis Schaeffer's little book *Art and the Bible* (1971) in my father's den and then I read H. R. Rookmaaker's *Modern Art and the Death of a Culture* (1971). And they confused me. The portrait of "modern art" that Rookmaaker and Schaeffer painted, which depicted a face distorted by spiritual poverty and aesthetic decadence, didn't resemble the one I had fallen in love with, which possessed such surprising beauty hewn through suffering, resonating so deeply with my experience of the Christian faith. However, when I vowed to correct that distorted and emaciated portrait, what I was really doing was responding to my own fears of devoting myself not only to the study of modern art as a specialist, as my profession, but my fear of allowing it to become a part of my inner life. What was I missing? Were Schaeffer and Rookmaaker right? What was wrong with me, spiritually and theologically, to be drawn to a cultural practice so universally dismissed by Christian thinkers? Could modern art destroy my faith?

Christian writing on modern art has been a consistent source of disappointment to me. It is not that the artists, philosophers, or theologians who write about it are wrong, although from my vantage point as a specialist, most have very little understanding of the history of art, especially modern art. Rather, the source of my disappointment is emotional. *I simply do not feel described by their sentences.* Their approach to modern art feels distant, at arm's length, and with their minds made up as to why it should be avoided or explained away.

My relationship with modern art was different. It had the agency—it led and I followed. And viewed through the probing binoculars of Schaeffer and Rookmaaker and that well-meaning elder, *it was illicit.* Modern art had put its hands on me—it was doing something to me. It wasn't something "out there" that nihilists or humanists or secularists were making or interpreting. It was in my house—we were doing something: wrestling, fighting, or making love. All I knew is that I wasn't staring at it from a distance, with the objectivity to pronounce once and for all on its vices. But how could I have admitted—to the church, to myself—that modern art and I had already consummated our relationship?

In retrospect I am thankful that I had the space to pursue my vocation as an art historian wonderfully unencumbered by those questions. I used to consider the particular brand of prairie anti-intellectualism and dispensational Christian community in which I was raised to be a curse—something I was glad to be rid of after discovering Calvin and Abraham Kuyper, as well as the deeper wells of the Catholic and Orthodox traditions. But now, tonight, I can consider it a providential gift. It allowed me to plunge into my craft and learn it for its own sake rather than merely as a means to make theological statements.

I do not oppose "the integration of faith and learning" or advocate keeping faith sealed off from the messiness of culture—quite the opposite, in fact. I do, however, resist the tendency to "apply" faith to culture, to art—as if paintings, poems, theatre performances, novels, and songs don't themselves do something to us, and do something theological. Rather than metaphors of application, integration, and connection, I prefer the metaphor of *conversation*, which respects the agency of art and implies a much more intimate relationship.

This sounds sacrilegious and incredibly impious, but Luther somewhere said that we are free to pursue our vocations as if God didn't exist. What an incredibly scandalous thing to say! But I feel what he meant. And it's liberating not to believe that God is looking over my shoulder as I scramble to offer an account of how what I do "transforms" culture, or is "kingdom work" or "redeems" the world. The Reformation tradition reveals that God doesn't need our good works. But our neighbor does. And so I felt, and still do, that the work I do as an art historian, curator, art critic, and teacher is simply a manifestation of loving my neighbor. In this case, my neighbor was an artist who worked in New York in 1950 or Paris in 1900 or is working now in Los Angeles. But the works they produced are also my neighbors, whom I love and serve by listening to them.

My life as a Christian, as one who hears God's promises of life and tries to respond in faith, has been inseparably woven into my relationship with modern art. My lack of interest in Christian approaches to modern art is that they simply don't have any skin in the game. I don't feel that they *need* the arts, that their faith in Christ somehow needs this poem, that play or song, or this painting. Their sentences don't possess the urgency and bear the weight of having struggled, fought, loved modern art *from the inside*, as a partner, neighbor, lover. I felt responsible to those artists, dead and alive, and for those paintings that have so much to say, and to the writers, curators, and collectors who devoted their lives to them.

With apologies to Josh Ritter, I had a "Girl in the War," and if they couldn't help me find a way to help her, they could go to hell.

In Rilke's famous poem entitled "The Archaic Greek Torso of Apollo," the narrator is confronted by a marble statue, which speaks. It says, "You must change your life!" The work of art makes a claim on the viewer—you whom I see, you who stands before me—you must give an account. *And I felt that claim.* Theologian Oswald Bayer simply but provocatively states, "we must be told who we are."[3] A painting does something like that to us—it diagnoses us, telling us who we are, telling us through paint that we will die. And one of the ways it does so is by disclosing the present. As sons and daughters of Cain, we live our lives as restless wanderers, enveloped in a fog of discontent. We find comfort in the past with our nostalgia or regret—and in the future with our fears and ambitions. A work of art jerks us out of that fog and back into the present moment. The painting, when I happen upon it at a museum, exists at that moment, for me. I am the intended audience for that work. And it speaks to me. What do I hear?—that is the challenge and opportunity of art criticism. And that is where I live and breathe and have my being. In his book *The Wound of Knowledge*, Rowan Williams writes,

> To be absorbed in the sheer otherness of any created order or beauty is to open the door to God, because it involves that basic displacement of the dominating ego without which there can be no spiritual growth.[4]

A painting is that kind of open door for me. Every conversation I have with an artist, Christian or (usually) not, is a theological conversation. But there isn't much writing out there on art in general or modern art in particular from a Christian or theological perspective that reflects on the claim that it makes on the viewer. What usually matters, for both writers inside and outside the church, is the artist's world view, his or her beliefs or the work of art's capacity to illumine historical context, or a million other things that distract us from this isolating encounter. Yet I agree with both T. S. Eliot and Oscar Wilde. Eliot once said that the meaning of a poem lies somewhere between the poem and the reader. And in his brilliant dialogue, "The Critic as Artist" (1891), Wilde states, "For when the work is finished it has, as it were, an independent life of its own, and may deliver a message far other than that which was put into its lips to say."[5] My own experience confers the truth of Wilde's claim. I know artists who profess atheism with their lips, yet make paintings that confess otherwise. It is also my experience that self-described Christian artists make paintings that say something else entirely.

Burdened with the desire to justify my relationship with modern art to the church, feeling that I owed it to Schaeffer, Rookmaaker, Wolterstorff,

---

3. Bayer, *Freedom in Response*, 54.
4. Williams, *The Wound of Knowledge*, 213.
5. Wilde, "The Critic as Artist," 202.

Seerveld, and others, I wrote a book entitled *God in the Gallery: A Christian Embrace of Modern Art*, which was published by Baker Academic in 2008 while I was the Chief Curator of the Sheldon Museum of Art. I argued that the problem was not with modern art, but with the kind of Christianity that was brought to bear on it. In response, I offered a Christian tradition that was shaped by a larger Nicene tradition, especially through the tradition of the icon as well as liturgical and sacramental practices as a way to give modern art, and my passion for it, theological and aesthetic space to breathe, to speak.

But in retrospect, it did not matter what theological tradition I was accessing. In the end, *I was trying to justify modern art to myself.* If I could do so, perhaps I could claim it as a legitimate relationship—I could once and for all make an honest spouse of modern art, *to reconcile* my faith and my vocation—reconcile myself to myself.

But I stand before you incapable of justifying my relationship with modern art, theologically or otherwise. All I can do is confess that I cannot imagine my life as a human or as a Christian without it; that it has made a claim on me, and that God has graciously worked through that claim.

The tradition of modern art, beginning with Gustave Courbet in the nineteenth century and extending into the present, establishes the artist's studio as a legitimate place for a human being to paint their way into their identity—through their faith, disbelief, hopes, and fears. In the studio they stand before themselves, the world, and God. Unhinged from the necessity of understanding their work as the fulfillment of commissions, they were free (or, as Sartre observes, condemned) to define the trajectory of their own work, through their own felt experience—to create their own significance, to invent their own roles as artists and the function of their artifacts as a means to give meaning to their lives. Free to do *anything* in the artist's studio, the modern artist has a responsibility to do *something*. The modern tradition in art is thus the accumulation of these remarkable *somethings*, disclosing the human condition in particularly powerful and distinctive ways, as art becomes a means for self-discovery. Edvard Munch encapsulated this approach to the studio when he said, "in my art I attempt to explain life and its meaning to myself," an attempt to paint the "soul's diary."[6] Yet "self-discovery" and the creation of meaning is not a private affair, but always consists of the artist's relationship to the world and to God—even if "God" is only an echo, a ghost that haunts his consciousness. As Oswald Bayer reminds us, "knowledge of God and knowledge of self are not to be separated."[7]

---

6. Prideaux, *Edvard Munch*, 35.

7. Bayer, *A Contemporary in Dissent*, 48.

The result of this self-discovery in the studio is pain—the pain of separation, alienation, loneliness, and death. Edvard Munch, whose picture *The Scream*, which sold for $120 million and who after his death became a national hero in his native Norway, once said "Art emerges from joy and pain," and then he added, "Mostly from pain."[8] And this seems to me one of the important lessons of modern art: it reminds us of something we want to forget—our suffering, our vulnerability, and our weakness. At the deepest levels, it is the emaciated figures of Munch rather than the heroism of Michelangelo's titans or the beauty of Raphael's angels that connects with us. If we let it, Munch's wound connects with our wound. We must, as J. G. Hamann observed, be led by God into the hell of self-knowledge and out again. We need to be killed and then raised from the dead. Somehow, a painting by Monet, Cézanne, or Picasso touches that fear and hope—or at least that is what *I* hear and feel in their work. Modern art puts us back in touch with our pain and suffering, which is where art meets us, where God meets us, for we are all like Melville's Ahab: "gnawed within and scorched without."[9] If we let it, Munch's wound connects to our wound. And it is only there, in our vulnerability, misery, and anger, that God meets us. And, east of Eden, it is only through this suffering and fear that we can experience beauty, goodness, and truth. Francis Bacon once said about his vocation, "I painted to be loved." Do you hear the pain and vulnerability in that sentence, from one of the most wealthy and powerful artists of the twentieth century? The tradition of modern art reminds us that all human creative work comes from the desire to be loved for who we are and the pain of not receiving that.

Modern art contradicts our desire to cover up this wound. It reminds us who we are in part by reminding us that there is a lot more at stake in art than representing classical stories and biblical narratives, in shaping virtue and teaching morality through images. It wrestles with our tendency to make our beliefs about ourselves and our world the center of the cosmos, to make ourselves the subjects of our existential sentences, to be, as David Foster Wallace said, "lords of our tiny skull-sized kingdoms."[10] And we want our visual imagery to feed our old Adam's desire to shape the world around our own beliefs and our own desires—to make art fit into our world view, decorate our own psychic interiors.

Modern art pushes against this. It lives in discontinuities. It contradicts our belief that artistic value is found in technical virtuosity, that its "meaning" should declare itself immediately, that looking is easy, and art

8. Quoted in Tøjner, *Munch in His Own Words*, 135.
9. Melville, *Moby-Dick*, 158.
10. Wallace, *This is Water*, 117.

is about comforting us with what's familiar. It's a stick shoved into the relentlessly spinning spokes of our incessantly spinning desire for emotional, intellectual, and aesthetic efficiency.

And it has taught me some things about my faith. Christianity is not a life system, helping me make sense of the world, making it transparent and explainable. In fact, it often makes the world more impenetrable, mysterious, and frustrating to me, creating discontinuities and sharp edges that confuse and anger me. In *My Bright Abyss*, Christian Wiman observes:

> If God is a salve applied to unbearable psychic wounds, or a dream figure conjured out of memory and mortal terror, or an escape from a life that has become either too appalling or too banal to bear, then I have to admit: it is not working for me.[11]

And he continues, "I never truly felt the pain of unbelief until I began to believe."[12]

It seems that faith in the promises of God's Word actually increases the *disparity* between the promise we hear—"I am with you always, even unto the end of the age"—and the world that we see: the sickness, death, and injustice. The gospel actually opens up a space for lamentation, for anger, for dismay, for crying out—why? That is the question I often hear in modern art. Ironically, it reminds me that a painting is more than meets the eye, and that we live by faith, not by sight (2 Cor 5:7), that appearances, even painted appearances, can deceive.

And so as I have learned to lean into my passion for modern art without the protection of a "Christian world view" and free of the burden of justifying it theologically, I have discovered paths rich for theological reflection. Luther believed that theology did not consist merely of true statements about God, but was bound up in a divine-human relationship: the God who justifies and the sinful human being. Therefore, theology is always already interwoven with the troubled conscience of the one doing it, the one who stands before God and the world and knows he or she must give an account. For Luther, theology included what he called *tentatio*, or "agonizing struggle," and so was always mindful of the sinful person with a troubled conscience who stands before a justifying God.[13]

When my eye catches a painting on the wall in a museum, it addresses me and opens up a space between us, a space in which I am rendered receptive and responsive. Luther countered the traditional scholastic distinction

11. Wiman, *My Bright Abyss*, 9.

12. Ibid., 12.

13. See Bayer, *Theology the Lutheran Way*, 42–65; Bayer, *Martin Luther's Theology*, 29–43.

between theory and practice, between the *vita contemplatio* and *vita acteo* with the *vita passiva*, or the receptive life, which responds in faith.[14] Strikingly, justification by faith, which is often reduced to a soteriological metaphor, is, in Luther's thought, the very definition of a human being, describing the very reality of human existence itself.[15] The human being, as Oswald Bayer observes, "stands in the dative case," one whose existence and identity has been given, and one for whom the basic human response is faith.[16]

An encounter with a painting hanging on the wall of a museum is an aesthetic reminder of our receptivity, passivity, and responsibility, activating that theological reality in which you and I stand before the face of another, whether it is our neighbor, ourselves, or God. And it brings to the fore the importance of faith. An encounter with a painting is a reminder that I live before the face of others: before the face of God, the face of my neighbor, and even before myself. It actualizes the present, where I usually refuse to live, since my troubled conscience drifts to the past in nostalgia or regret or lurches into the future in either fear or aspiration. To be addressed by a painting is to become exquisitely aware that we are addressed now, at this moment, that there is nothing we have that we did not first receive (1 Cor 4: 7). That painting that addresses me, arrests my attention, and makes a claim on me, can do so only because I have been first called into existence, because my human freedom is not, as Oswald Bayer said, my echo, but a response.[17]

But Christ doesn't make everything fit together, so we can sing that same song that made Sam Phillips cringe. My experience, and I am willing to bet it is yours as well, is that you're lying in a gutter somewhere dying, and the Christ that you confess there is a Christ you can only respond to in faith, which, as Luther says quite wonderfully, is "a living, daring confidence in God's grace, so sure and certain that a man would stake his life on it a thousand times."[18] Modern art has often forced me to take leaps of faith, leaps from which I continue to fall. Yet they are leaps I would take again and again. Leaps no doubt I will take again and again.

> She'll tear a hole in you, the one you can't repair
> But I still love her, I don't really care.
>
> —The Lumineers, "Stubborn Love"

---

14. Bayer, *Martin Luther's Theology*, 42–43.

15. See "The Disputation Concerning Man," thesis no. 32.

16. Bayer, "The Ethics of Gift," 447.

17. Bayer, *Freedom in Response*, 54.

18. Luther, "Definition of Faith."

One of the questions I fear, and I have feared it with ever-more intensity over the last few years, is "What do you do?" And as my life circumstances have changed, I've deflected it in different ways. I've said, "I'm an art museum curator" or "I'm an art history professor," or "I run a studio for an artist in Miami." And then more recently, I've said, "I'm the Director of Theological and Cultural Practices at Coral Ridge Presbyterian Church."

But my vocation, what I have been called to suffer, is to love modern art. God made me to look at and think about paintings. And no matter what institutional location I receive a paycheck from or the title on my business card, my relationship to modern art remains the same.

Not long ago, faced with what I can only describe as a vocational crisis, I escaped to New York City to look at some paintings by Paul Cézanne at the Museum of Modern Art. At that time, it was all I could think of doing. This is not exactly the kind of behavior one would expect from an evangelical on staff at a conservative Presbyterian church in South Florida.

But these paintings of Cézanne and I have a history. We first met when I was a graduate student. I initially considered his clunky landscapes, sloping still lifes, and thick bathers to be nothing but bridges to abstraction, an awkward but necessary transition from Monet to the defiant black squares of Malevich or the tragic gestures of Pollock. If they were important for me, they were only so historically, as I was figuring out the tradition of modern art.

But others, like Monet, Rodin, Rilke, and Heidegger, whom I was devouring at the time, thought otherwise: "If only one could think as directly," Heidegger said, "as Cézanne paints."[19] In 1899 the young artist Henri Matisse purchased a strange little painting of Cézanne's at great financial sacrifice.

In an interview in 1925 Matisse, long after he had achieved international acclaim, confessed:

> If you only knew the moral strength, the encouragement that his remarkable example gave me all my life! In moments of doubt, when I was searching for myself, frightened sometimes by my discoveries, I thought: "If Cézanne is right, I am right." And I knew that Cézanne had made no mistake.[20]

Matisse continued, "It has sustained me morally in the critical moments of my venture as an artist . . . I have drawn from it my faith and perseverance."

I remember asking myself at the time, *What am I missing?*

19. Quoted in Danchev, *Cézanne*, 356.
20. Quoted in ibid., 15.

According to the poet Rilke, this was not an unusual question. "For a long time nothing," Rilke writes about Cézanne's canvases, "and suddenly one has the right eyes."[21]

The "right eyes" did not come to me in graduate school. They came as I began to work closely with artists over the next few years, to sit with them in their studios, watch them work, and reflect on our conversations. It happened as I wrote about paintings, organized exhibitions, and instructed students. And perhaps most importantly, it happened as I experienced the struggle to remain faithful to my vocation, to what took me to New York to study modern art in the first place. It happened in the midst of professional challenges and personal responsibilities, involving much more than paintings.

The right eyes came as I suffered as a human being and experienced failure as a husband, father, son, friend, and art historian. They came as I witnessed similar suffering and failure in the lives of the artists about whom I cared so deeply. The "right eyes" came when I looked at Cézanne's paintings and saw them as artifacts made by a human being who suffered his vocation, suffered his artistic project, struggling with doubt his entire life. In fact, the right eyes came just a few months ago, after twenty-one years of marriage, three teenaged children, and a radical and ultimately disastrous move from Nebraska to South Florida. (My wife and children have been implicated in my relationship with modern art—their own lives touched by it—enduring not only long periods of my emotional infidelity but also have having their worlds forever changed by decisions I've made for its sake.)

What was Cézanne's artistic project?

His single artistic goal, *which is also the driving aspiration for the tradition of modern art*, was to paint nature as he experienced it, as he received it, "*sur le motif*," as he would say—that is, out in the landscape where he would set up his easel.

The results were surprising, to say the least. And he experienced significant opposition from the academic establishment.

Amidst the insecurities and doubt, the resistance and misunderstanding, he painted until the day he died, after having contracted an illness while being caught in a thunderstorm when he was painting *sur le motif*. He made 954 paintings, 645 watercolors, and 1,400 drawings over the span of his lifetime. He rose at 4 a.m. and was either in his studio or *sur le motif* by 7 a.m. every day.

Cézanne was a servant to the world around him, looking and studying and ultimately reveling in the wonder and mystery of what was given to

21. Rilke, *Letters on Cézanne*, 39.

him. He would sit for hours staring into the landscape with no movement, "lizard-like," as observers called it. They said that it could be twenty minutes to an hour between brushstrokes. While his establishment colleagues in the Academy painted mythical figures, gods and goddesses, cherubs and putti, "elevating" the imagination of the viewer toward God through "beauty," Cézanne dwelt in his and our creatureliness, feet firmly planted on the ground. Many of his admirers claimed that his greatest gift was to paint the weight of his subjects, whether it was a head, house, or oak tree. One hostile critic said that Cézanne could even paint bad breath.

Cézanne's art—indeed the tradition of modern art within which he painted—reminds us we live our lives *sur le motif*. We are always "in it," that is, in the terrible beauty, suffering, and frightening givenness of the world, as our stomachs churn and our minds race. Heidegger said that Cézanne's paintings declare one thing: "life is terrifying."

And yet, Cézanne's paintings also say something else.

Although the world is full of pain, suffering, and doubt, if we allow ourselves to sit still, perhaps lizard-like, and look closely enough, we can hear something else, something real—a song.

In an essay on the Russian poet Anna Akhmatova, Joseph Brodsky wrote, "Love is essentially an attitude maintained by the infinite toward the finite. The reversal constitutes either faith or poetry."[22]

I'm not exactly sure what I was doing at MoMA looking at those odd paintings by Cézanne a few months ago, but I think I was, like Matisse, looking for faith and perseverance. And, standing before you tonight, I think I can say that I found it.

So, who's afraid of modern art?

I am.

And I am learning to thank God for it. Thank you.

---

22. Brodsky, *Less Than One*, 44.

1

THE EAR

The ear is the only organ of a Christian.

—MARTIN LUTHER

As all the Heavens were a Bell,
And Being, but an Ear.

—EMILY DICKINSON

In the space between hearing and speaking, being judged and judging, we find ourselves in this world not in some harmony that has already been achieved, but in the midst of a battle of controversies and conflicting interpretations.

—OSWALD BAYER

HEARING *THE SCREAM*

On a recent visit to New York I went to see *The Scream* (1895), a little drawing in pastel by Edvard Munch on loan to the Museum of Modern Art from a private collector. It is one of four versions that the artist made of the famous subject, which consists of a genderless figure, standing on a bridge, holding its hairless head and screaming. The image of the silent scream has entered our popular visual culture, from coffee mugs to Macaulay Culkin's trademark expression in the movie *Home Alone*.[1] It hangs in a custom-built display wall in the center of a room, amidst other drawings, prints, and paintings by the Norwegian artist. Tourists crowd in front of the little pastel to pose in their version of the famous gesture.

It didn't look like a masterpiece. It looked vulnerable and weak, suffocating amidst the spectacle it had caused, on display in a way it was never intended to be. And I thought of the artist, whose life was indelibly marked by the death of his older sister, Sophia, when he was a boy, who kept the chair she died in with him until the day he died, and who, late in life, painted full-length portraits of men he admired, calling them "guardians," which he leaned up against walls in his house to protect him and keep him company during those long nights of sleeplessness. And I thought of the artist who said, "in my art I attempt to explain life and its meaning to myself."[2]

And I thought of the disparity between this little picture's notoriety and the artist's pain, the spectacle of culture as entertainment and painting as a way for one man to live, or perhaps better put, for one man to remain alive.

The 120 Million-Dollar Question

This little pastel drawing that cowers embarrassingly in the middle of the room at MoMA last spring fetched the highest price ever paid for a work of art at public auction, nearly $120 million. The visitors came to gawk at *that*—to see what $120 million looked like. But *The Scream* raises a $120 million question. Is it worth it? Is any painting worth it, much less one that looks as poorly drawn and sloppily painted as this one?

Modern art is strange and intimidating, and it puts you on the spot. It appears to play by a different set of rules than the "art" we're used to seeing. It hangs in art museums throughout the world, but we're not quite sure how

1. For more information on Munch, see Sue Prideaux, *Edvard Munch*; Ann Temkin, *Edvard Munch*; and Elizabeth Prelinger, *After the Scream*.

2. Quoted in Prideaux, *Edvard Munch*, 35.

it got there, to be frank. Some of the most creative and progressive culture makers, including artists and curators in the art world, are still not quite sure what to make of it.

But before you follow the crowd out of the gallery, let's linger a little while longer in front this odd little picture that has received so much attention.

Listening and Seeing

In an essay, "On Painting," artist Enrique Martínez Celaya writes, "a painting often distracts us by what it looks like."[3] Is it possible that a painting, of all things, can be more than meets the eye? Martínez Celaya's observation reflects an important biblical truth, one that Luther recovered from St. Paul: our eyes deceive us. We live by faith, not by sight (2 Cor 5: 7).

We are easily impressed with visual displays of power, wealth, and beauty, and we are eager to see God's presence in them. The old Adam in us is a theologian of glory, who wants to see God fulfilling our desires, completing our natures, helping us ascend to his presence. But if our eyes deceive us, what are we to do in front of a painting?

Let me suggest that we follow Luther's advice and listen. Luther claimed that the ears are the only organs of a Christian, for it is through the ears that we hear God's promise, his promise to love us, to be with us, to never forsake us, to be for us in spite of what we see before our eyes and even in spite of his hiddenness—our inability to see God amidst suffering, pain, and injustice. By hearing God's Word, we live by faith, not by sight. For Luther, this is what it means to be a theologian of the cross.[4] But how do we listen to a painting?

To listen to a work of art requires a moment of passivity, of receptivity that allows the work of art to be active, to allow it to speak, like Rilke's archaic Greek torso, to make a claim on us. A work of art has agency and to listen to it allows it, as literary critic George Steiner once said, to have the run of our inner chambers.

But we like our art—and our religion—visually pleasing. We like it practical, useful, maybe a little therapeutic. We want to be active, so we can use art and religion for our own purposes—to elevate, empower, and even entertain us. We want our Jesus, like our art, to help us succeed in our life projects, which, following St. Paul and Luther, are centered on securing our justification. We live our lives in search of what Hegel called "mutual

---

3. Martínez Celaya, "On Painting," in *Collected Writings*, 242.
4. See Gerhard Forde, *On Being a Theologian of the Cross.*

recognition." John Locke even claimed that "person" is a "forensic term," that is, defined by public trial. Oswald Bayer observes:

> Throughout our lives we continually seek to find excuses for the fact that we live as we do, that we are existent rather than non-existent, and that we are as we are and not something different.[5]

And so we enlist art and religion into this project of self-justification, of self-recognition. You and I, if we're honest with ourselves, gravitate toward a theology that resembles Joel Osteen and art that resembles a Thomas Kinkade painting much more closely than we care to admit. This is not because we're ignorant about art and theology. It is because we're human, and we believe we only need some help here and there. We're drawn to what looks like piety, improvement, progress, and talent. We are drawn, like moths to the light, to what Luther called theologies of glory, those theologies that want to see God working visibly in ways we value (beauty, wealth, strength). And because it is so powerful visually, a painting is one of those cultural artifacts that is most susceptible to those seductions. Yet a painting is more than meets the eye. A painting is actually a silly thing. And it requires faith.

But Jesus tells us that we don't need a little help. We need to be killed and then raised from the dead. Sometimes I think that one of art's most important responsibilities is to kill us, to kill our confidence in ourselves and our understanding of the world.

Modern art contradicts most of our assumptions about art. It isn't about heroes to emulate and challenge us, relaxing scenes with happy trees and quaint cottages to comfort us, outrageous images that entertain or scandalize us, or even expressions of an artist's "world view." And because it pushes against our expectations and assumptions, modern art can offer a fresh way of reflecting on how God is at work in the world through his two words, law and gospel, a word the kills and a word that makes alive, in surprising and often scandalous ways, even in the Museum of Modern Art.

Weak and Vulnerable

The artist Mark Rothko once said that it is a risky business to send a painting out into the world. And let's be honest, smearing smelly pigment across a scrap of canvas with a brush is a rather strange endeavor. In spite of the fact that they hang in the Louvre and the Metropolitan Museum of Art or cost collectors millions of dollars, paintings—even the so-called

5. Bayer, *Living by Faith*, 3.

masterpieces—are weak and vulnerable things, always seemingly subject to destruction, ridicule, misunderstanding—or, perhaps worst, neglect.

To devote one's life to painting pictures at all is an absurd practice, one that seems to fly in the face of what the world finds important, relevant, or useful. It contradicts both non-Christian and Christian theologies of culture, which are often obsessed with consumption, education, redemption, or transformation (going from good to great)—theologies that work hard to make painting fit into the justifying, transactional power schemes that shape the world in which both Christians and non-Christians live and breathe and have their being. Paintings exist as contradictions to the conditional engine that drives the world.

Nature and the Modern Artist

Edvard Munch, like so many modern artists, understood an important theological point: nature is much more than meets the eye. In 1907 Munch wrote in his journal:

> Nature is not only that which is visible to the eye. It is also the inner image of the mind. The images upon the reverse of the eye.[6]

This might come as a surprise, but modern artists rediscovered the awesome wonder of nature, a nature they observed from outside and felt within. One of the reasons that Munch despised academic painting—the pictures of nymphs, nudes, angels, and heroes that populated the salons and academies of his day—was its presentation of an overly explained, interpreted, and allegorized nature. For Munch, nature was mysterious, brilliantly opaque, dangerously violent, and put insurmountable pressure on body and soul. He perceived in nature something terrible and unrelenting: *it demands our life*. The modern artist doesn't "interpret" nature; he wrestles with it. Paul Cézanne, one of the most influential artists in the history of modernism, even admitted, "Nature appears to me so complicated."[7]

Art and Death

That Munch said that art comes "mostly from pain" makes us wince. We want art to be uplifting, inspirational, and much of what we get with modern

6. Quoted in Tøjner, *Munch in His Own Words*, 131

7. Quoted in Danchev, *Cézanne*, 258.

art is angst, pain, and weakness, all of which seems to make of humanity not a little but a lot less than the angels. This contradicts our inner theologian of glory, who bristles at weakness and failure and pain in art, which reminds us of our own weakness and failure and pain. But Munch would have none of it.

Munch grows old in his paintings, his eyesight fails, he loses his virility, he experiences the death of loved ones, drifts sleeplessly around his home lonely and afraid, dwelling in the growing isolation and desperation of a modern life in which even the most routine daily tasks have the potential to ignite into violent confrontations with his deepest fears.

Indelibly scarred as a bed-ridden and sickly child by the death of his oldest sister, whom he worshiped, Munch's work is a confrontation with death and the pain of loss. One of the pictures on display at MoMA is a lithograph of his sister on her deathbed. Munch recounted that his sister, in a burst of energy, rose from her bed to sit in a chair, where she died. Munch kept that chair with him for the rest of his life. When he died, it was in his studio.

Many shocked viewers, presuming that art's role is to entertain or teach, found Munch's confrontation with death, illness, and weakness sickening. And it is.

Be Opened!

In the Gospel of Mark, Jesus heals a man born deaf and mute in a manner that recalls the mystery of creation:

> And taking him aside from the crowd privately, he put his fingers into his ears, and after spitting touched his tongue. And looking up to heaven, he sighed and said to him, "Ephphatha," that is, "Be opened" (Mark 7:33–34).

On September 8, 1538, Martin Luther preached a remarkable sermon on this text. For Luther, Christ comes to open our ears so that we may be able to hear his Word in the world. As Oswald Bayer observes about this sermon, "The whole world is filled with speaking" but, through sin, "the whole world is deaf!"[8] But without Christ's life-giving Word, "Ephphatha," we hear nothing but the sound of death, the sound of our own anxiety. Bayer continues,

> The most surprising point in the entire sermon is that Luther, without digressing and in a theologically bold way that is most strange to our ears, takes the Word that Jesus Christ himself

8. Bayer, *Martin Luther's Theology*, 107.

speaks in the miracle story and claims it as a Word that every creature speaks to us. For Luther, this means that Jesus Christ is so powerful when he speaks his Word that he discloses the entire world to us.[9]

Our ears are our first organs. The world, which existed as brute, unyielding nature, is returned to us to receive as a gift through hearing the promises of God's Word. The world, which pours forth speech (Ps 19:2), is given to us in all its sensory wonder.

What do I hear in *The Scream*?

Silence.

This is what I have written in previous iterations of this essay, and after looking at the painting and reflecting on it further, my answer is different. What do I hear now?

My scream.

Munch as a Theologian of the Cross

The Scream appears at first glance to be deaf and mute, in part because we want to see it as Munch's anxiety, a product of his particular neurosis. And Munch certainly knew that his paintings were silent, and it terrified him. About the origins of this work, Munch remembers, as he stood on a pier, "I felt a huge endless scream course through nature."[10] Yet *The Scream*, which he painted four times, something he often did with subjects that preoccupied him, is an attempt to externalize that fear that plagued him, the fear that no one could hear him scream, that what coursed through nature actually coursed through his veins, and his alone. For Munch nature became an echo chamber where his own anxiety in the face of death could only yield a desperate, silent scream. But *The Scream* is Munch's attempt to get out, to allow it to be heard, somehow, in paint and pastel. Later in life, sequestered in his large, empty home, he painted protection in the form of full-length portraits of his friends he called "guardians," which he stationed throughout the house to protect him as he wandered sleepless throughout the night.

The Scream is the sound of our response to nature's brute silence and indifference, undisclosed as gift through God's Word. This is not a nature that can be idealized, improved upon, or completed with a little dose of grace. *It needs to be recreated.* *The Scream* gives us what the hiddenness of

9. Ibid., 115.
10. Prideaux, *Edvard Munch*, 151.

God in paint sounds like, feels like, and looks like. *The Scream* does not edify or teach us. *It describes us, and then it kills us.*

Perhaps we reject Munch's paintings and those of other modern artists not because they look strange or express a "world view" or "values" at odds with our own, but because they confront us with our own mortality, our own weakness, failure, and impending death, which we then go to a museum or a church to forget. Luther said that the theologian of the cross has the courage to call a thing what it actually is. Munch shows us that life is defined by suffering, pain, and death.

We do not interpret *The Scream*. We feel it on the inside. It interprets us, interrogates us, it draws us out from the pack, where we often take solace, as part of the "difficulties" of life or part of the "human condition." This little picture triggers our anxiety, which lies barely under the surface, that I, and I alone, am the problem. *The Scream* forces us to recognize that this is not merely the product of a neurotic avant-garde artist, but a disclosure of who I am, which I work feverishly to cover up, often by going to museums to look at art to get some culture or to church to listen to sermons and get something spiritual.

This vulnerable little pastel, in its hermetically sealed silence, crowded by tourists in a museum in New York, calls a thing what it actually is. Can you hear it: the silent scream that pulses through your veins, which no one around you hears?

A Lament

And yet. It is tempting to see *The Scream*, like much of modern art, as a lament. As Oswald Bayer observes, a lament asks, in the face of pain, suffering, and injustice, "Is God keeping his promises?"[11] A lament, however, is only possible when the promises are known. And so *The Scream* can be heard as a lament by those who believe a promise, that there is a day after, that there will come a time when all our tears will be wiped away. Like all paintings, modern or otherwise, it yearns for a viewer who confesses, "all things were created through him and for him" (Col 1:16).

The Scream is not the *last* word. But, in its articulation of pain and suffering, in its diagnosis of our human condition—a condition that must be killed and then recreated, not merely improved upon—it must be the *first word* that we hear.

---

11. Bayer, *Living by Faith*, 69.

BEARING ARTISTIC WITNESS

It was Aleksandr Tvardovsky's habit to lounge about his apartment in his bathrobe looking at the manuscripts that littered his living quarters. As editor of the liberal magazine *Novy Mir* in the Soviet Union during the height of the Cold War, Tvardovsky was well known as a Soviet poet as well as a staunch defender of his literary magazine's independence. One morning he came upon a manuscript and began reading. He then stopped, put the manuscript down, took a shower, shaved, put on his best clothes, and drove to his office to finish reading it. The manuscript? It was *One Day in the Life of Ivan Denisovich,* by Aleksandr Solzhenitsyn, who wrote it in secret in the late 1950s. Tvardovsky was so moved by the manuscript that he convinced Khrushchev to publish it and it appeared in *Novy Mir* in serial form in 1962. Solzhenitsyn would go on to win the Nobel Prize for Literature several years later. The year 2012 marked the fiftieth anniversary of his work's publication.

It is easy to see how Solzhenitsyn is the hero of the story. But it is the editor Tvadovsky who recognized its brilliance amidst the clutter of competing manuscripts and fought for its publication, at great cost to his career and even his life. The poet Osip Mandelstam once said that the Russians take their poets seriously—they shoot them. (Mandelstam would himself experience their seriousness.) This story demonstrates the need for discerning critics, curators, and editors with the sensitivity to *recognize* significant artistic achievement and the *courage* to promote it, whatever the cost, within their spheres of influence. This is especially so in our isolated, distracted, and amnesic cultural moment, where quality and success are defined by the phrase "going viral," where *Jersey Shore* and Miley Cyrus dominate cultural discourse, where art dealers prowl undergraduate art departments on the coasts to find the twentysomethings with the next signature style. In an article published in 2011 in *The Economist*, Jeff Koons's new work is celebrated as "speak[ing] to a global elite that believes in the holy trinity of sex, art and money. Art collectors enjoy seeing themselves reflected in what they buy."[12] Great art, literature, and music, and other cultural works are being produced, but there are more distractions and clutter that obscure them, and more effort is needed to support them.

Evangelicals have been largely content to participate in culture in a narrow, negative, oppositional way, railing against art that supposedly undermines a "Christian world view," *obsessing* about four-letter words in music and nudity in movies. Yet we also possess a well-earned reputation for the production of mediocre-to-atrocious art and culture, from

---

12. Thornton, "Sexy Contemporary Antiquities."

Thomas Kinkade, Warner Sallman, and CCM to the *Left Behind* franchise, and countless artifacts from "Christian artists" that are nothing more than thinly veiled propaganda.

It is clearly not enough to make culture. All of us make culture—that is what we do, which Andy Crouch has brilliantly demonstrated in *Culture Making* (2008). Evangelicals have a responsibility to support *great* art and culture, to support art and culture that will last beyond the news cycle, the fall season, even the current generation of consumers. When asked what he would do today if he knew that the world would end tomorrow, Martin Luther responded, "I will plant an apple tree."

Apple trees have been planted throughout culture, apple trees like Solzhenitsyn's *One Day in the Life of Ivan Denisovich* that have taken years to cultivate, requiring care and commitment beyond gauging the number of "hits" or "shares," beyond licking one's finger and determining where the winds of fashion are blowing. Artists will continue to make significant work in the face of the noise and distractions. What are needed, however, are critics, editors, and curators like Tvardovsky who recognize them and are willing to cultivate their work at any cost because they believe in their significance as works of art, as artifacts that give form to our humanity.

The world of culture (art, music, literature, film) is overrun by transactional artists who are less concerned about their craft and its capacity to give shape to the human condition than in chasing recognition—wealth, fame, power—like Jeff Koons, Damien Hirst, Thomas Kinkade, and Jerry Jenkins, who use "art" and "literature" to flatter and patronize their consumers. Yet the world of culture is also overrun by transactional curators, editors, and critics who chase these entertainers, who use them or allow themselves to be used by them to satisfy their own desire to be justified through wealth, fame, or power. These curators, editors, and critics wouldn't be caught dead missing the current bandwagon or standing alone in support of a particular artist who appears out of step with current trends.

The contemporary cultural landscape needs Christian participation like never before. Not because art needs to be transformed, redeemed, or remade into something "Christian." In fact, the last thing culture needs is "Christian artists." But rather, art needs to be protected and preserved by critics, curators, and editors who care about it for its own sake, as a practice that deepens our humanity, and is committed to preserving the great traditions of painting, film, poetry, prose, and music because they are a vital means of human expression. Christians who care about the arts must colabor with anyone who shares their commitments. But perhaps it is Christians, who believe their identity is hidden in Christ, whose justification as human beings is defined by what Christ has done, not what they do, and thus (ideally) have the freedom to resist the urge to use art as instruments of fame and power, who can recognize and support art that reveals the truth of our condition, our brokenness, while at the same time testifying to the alien presence of grace rustling about in the world, which comes from beyond the hills. Authentic art is nothing less than an aesthetic testimony to the promise of grace, and as such, it deserves our utmost respect and our efforts to preserve it against forces that would distract us, especially those forces that come in the name of decency and moral values. We need to be artistic witnesses, willing to seek out and preserve authentic art, no matter where it is, and no matter how unpopular it might be to do so, bearing even the criticism we will surely receive from fellow Christians.

One Day in the Life of Ivan Denisovich exists in the world not only because one man had the courage to write it, but also because another man heard it, and then had the courage to find a way to publish it, to make it available to you and to me.

ART AND EXPLANATION

Susan Sontag has a point. In her well-known essay, "Against Interpretation" (1964), Sontag argues that the classical mimetic theory of art has created an unnecessary distinction between form and content, which modern (and now postmodern) theories have merely intensified. Interpretation presumes that art must have content that can be extracted for use outside the work.[13] Sontag writes, "Directed to art, interpretation means plucking a set of elements (the X, the Y, the Z, and so forth) from the whole work. The task of interpretation is virtually one of translation." In the hands of interpretation, art becomes, at best, merely the visual illustration of an idea equally and fully expressible through other means, an idea that can ultimately (and perhaps most clearly) be articulated verbally.

The implications are considerable for writing about art from a self-consciously Christian perspective. Christianity presumes a metanarrative, or an overarching unified story, in which "all things" are made through, and held together in, Christ (Col 1). One of the many tensions between art and the Christian faith is that art and metanarratives fight against one another. The work of art exists in the world in its own glorious singularity. The metanarrative is all encompassing. It is a unified world view, a framework within which everything has a place and everything makes sense. The role of art criticism, in this context, is to demonstrate how a work of art fits securely into this schema. For these interpretations, whether Marxist, Freudian,

---

13. Sontag, "Against Interpretation."

Formalist, or Neo-Calvinist, art is significant only insofar as it affirms and strengthens the metanarrative confessed by the interpreter.

What do metanarratives presume and why do works of art resist them?

Metanarratives are stories that presume The End. But they presume not only *that* there is such an End but also *how* particular works of art fit into it.

The consequences are dire. Art comes to possess its integrity only insofar as it can be used in an interpreter's metanarrative, grist for the interpreter's ideological mill. Art is deprived of its own integrity as a world-making and space-creating work, as an artifact of human intentionality that pushes back on our metanarrative urges to reconcile the past and the future, to make sense of it all from our vantage point. For Luther and Calvin, the human heart is an idol-making factory. It is just as accurate to say that the human heart is a metanarrative factory, churning out explanation after explanation, justification after justification, in labyrinthine stories in which we, of course, are the hero, our beliefs vindicated, and others (including works of art) simply become bit players in our own idolatrous epic performance.

For Lutheran theologian Oswald Bayer, this human tendency to explain, to find meaning, is the manifestation of the old Adam.

> In our time and space, with all its hopelessness and obscurities, we do not live by sight. Here and now it is only the old Adam with his justifying thinking that attempts a comprehensive theory of world history. The old Adam within us wants to find meaning; he is concerned to assure himself about the meaning of the whole.[14]

The danger is not holding a belief in the promise of whole, or The End. It is to "explain" that whole or End through the circumstances of art, through the circumstances of our lives, through what we see (a theology of glory) rather than what we hear and suffer (a theology of cross). Saints Paul and John write that it is in Christ that all things have their being, that through Christ all things are made, and that Christ is working to make all things new. "All things" includes specific works of art. But the temptation is to confuse the mysterious unity of God's story with our cheap and idolatrous versions, rushing too hastily to make a work of art work *for me*, the interpreter, under the guise of a "Christian interpretation," when in reality such interpretation is really my own justification. (The temptation to make the work of art function as a tool for my own justifying work is a constant presence for the critic, as much for the Marxist as it is for the Neo-Kuyperian.) To enlist art into my own justifying efforts risks depriving the work of art of what it can

14. Bayer, *Living by Faith*, 35.

be, that is, a harbinger of a "deeper magic" at work in the world, the magic of grace. Unfortunately, what often happens in Christian art education or theology and the arts can become an idolatrous worship of a particular ideology or metanarrative which art is enlisted to support (i.e., the Christian world view) and grace is forgotten, as is the radical discontinuity between our experience (what we see) and our hope (what we believe), as well as the integrity of each individual work of art. It is well to remember what the great friend and critic of Kant, J. G. Hamann, said about our work: we weave only on "the underside of the carpet"[15]—we do not enjoy God's perspective on what constitutes the common good, human flourishing, or other ways of describing God's hidden work, amidst the suffering and pain that we observe and try to ignore.

As the Bible reveals, especially with Job, Jonah, and the other prophets, God is a moving target. His overwhelming love and grace cannot be explained and interpreted. The Spirit blows where it may. While we might affirm the Christian metanarrative as an act of faith, that in Christ all things are being made new, how it is being written is God's work, not ours.

And this is a source of great freedom. As Bayer continues,

> Faith frees us from this concern [the meaning of the whole]. It enables us to accept the finitude of our lives and of the many histories into which they are interwoven in the battle for justification, the life-and-death struggle for recognition. We can accept our finitude, yet still with sorrow and melancholy, lamenting our transitoriness.[16]

Art helps us live in the moment without having to explain it, to find "meaning" in it, to find how God is "at work" in our lives and explain his purposes. The responsibility of the Christian critic is to preserve that distinctive space that art can create, a space that allows us to feel his grace, which only exists and comes to us in the present moment, a glorious moment that needs no interpretation, explanation, or justification.

ROBERT HUGHES, JACKSON POLLOCK, AND ME

The art critic creates space for works of art to breathe. This task is difficult because he or she must use one medium of expression (words) to communicate the significance of another medium of expression (paint). Moreover,

---

15. Quoted in Betz, *After Enlightenment*, 95.
16. Bayer, *Living by Faith*, 35.

a painting by its very nature fights against words, defies words, undermines the capacity of words to make sense of it.

Yet the art critic's task is necessary. It is necessary because a painting is more complex than we assume. Every day we are bombarded with images that are produced to catch our distracted attention for only the briefest of moments. Because a painting, unlike a poem or a piece of music, makes itself present to us all at once, we want to treat it like all the other images we see around us on television, on the Internet, and on billboards. But the art critic exists to remind us that a painting, like a poem or a piece of music, unfolds over time, that it cannot be treated like other imagery. It demands our full intellectual and imaginative effort. A painting is much, much more than what hits our retina. And so the art critic's necessary task is to make us stop in front of it, to look more closely, think more actively, and imagine more widely. The art critic's responsibility is to remind us that painting operates in a world in which the slightest visual distinction carries monumental importance. The impossibility of this task is the tension of the critic's use of words to create space that allows a painting to breathe without words. The critic's words are disposable, like Wittgenstein's ladder. They are useful only as means to get us to a place where words are not necessary.

Art criticism is thus a difficult, if not impossible, task. And so the art critic is in constant jeopardy of overstepping his or her bounds, using words to limit rather than expand the work of art's expressive scope, reducing it to a visual illustration of some theory or idea; or drowning the work in discourse. The Abstract Expressionist painter Willem de Kooning once said that a critic came by his studio for fifteen minutes and then wrote a review that took him all day to read. Yet the danger exists that the art critic can make the work of art too accessible, too "easy" to apprehend, comprehend.

Many art critics recoil from this almost-impossible challenge. Robert Hughes, however, was one of those rare critics who understood exactly what was at stake.[17] Although I had read his work, it wasn't until I saw him in action that I truly began to appreciate his vision.

I was standing outside the Museum of Modern Art in New York in 1998 with about three other people the day before a monumental Jackson Pollock exhibition was to open.[18] A colleague at Christie's had given me access to a private VIP walk-through of the exhibition with about half a dozen other people. As I was waiting for the guards to open the door, Robert Hughes, with a copy of *The New York Times* tucked under his arm and a cup of coffee in his free hand, stopped at the front door as well. He was meeting

17. See Hughes, *American Visions*.
18. Varnedoe et al., *Jackson Pollock*.

someone. And that someone was Salman Rushdie, whose public presence at that time was extremely rare, since he had been the subject of a *fatwa* by the Ayatollah Khomeini in the late '80s for his controversial novel, *The Satanic Verses*.

I followed them throughout the exhibition as Hughes talked to Rushdie about Pollock's background, his influences, and how he understood the role of painting. As he walked the curious writer through his artistic development, and answered Rushdie's often puzzled questions along the way, I realized that this tour was the essence of Hughes's art criticism and the goal of all art criticism. He takes the reader on a tour, a tour of the artist's work, but also a tour of his thinking about the work. We read Hughes or any other art critic not only to gain an understanding of art, but also to gain an understanding of the critic, what he or she is thinking about, engaging or struggling with. Hughes had been wrestling with Pollock's paintings for decades and he was allowing Rushdie into that relationship, giving him a sense of that pressure, that tension, that experience, allowing Pollock's work to get Rushdie in a choke hold, and then showing him how to respond in order to transform a potential fight into a graceful dance.

As they shook hands and parted ways, it was clear that Hughes had converted Rushdie. He had transformed confusion into understanding. He had shown Rushdie the grace of Pollock's elegant paintings hewn from his tragic and painful life. Hughes had given both Pollock's paintings and Rushdie something only he could give: space to breathe.

2

THE AUDIENCE

The human being is human only as a listening being.

—OSWALD BAYER

Speak, that I may see you!

—J. G. HAMANN

FREE TO RECEIVE

Let's face it: Christians can be a pretty nervous and grumpy lot when it comes to art and culture. We're perpetually on the lookout for artistic evidence to prove that *this* is the most evil of generations. In fact, it seems as if many of us delight in being offended so that we can crow about the good old days when the church was the patron of the arts and bemoan the aesthetic consequences of the Enlightenment, modernity, and postmodernity.

A trip to the library, museum, art gallery, concert hall, or film theatre can become an occasion for worry and hand-wringing about what is "appropriate." And so we tend to categorize art and other cultural artifacts negatively, that is, the only positive category is the harmful or inappropriate one. This is a heavy burden to bear. And so it's understandable that we're a little foggy on what to enjoy, or even if a Christian is supposed to "enjoy" art at all. So, we tiptoe gingerly around it, limiting its use to covert evangelistic or political ops or as overt didactic tools to shape virtue, which really end up merely affirming bourgeois morality and indulging the desires of late capitalistic consumerism.

The most progressive of us are merely those who find less art and culture offensive than others. (Even among the artistically inclined and creative types in the church, modern art often remains incomprehensible.) Most Christians desire to make "our own art and culture," producing Christian artists, filmmakers, writers, and the like who can "take back" the culture, redeem it, transform it, or otherwise do something "Christian" to it.

But the world does not need more (or any) "Christian artists."

What the world does need, and needs desperately, are Christians who embrace our freedom in Christ to such a degree that we can listen to and participate in the art and culture that is at hand. What the world needs are more *listeners*, more *receivers*. The world needs us to pay attention to the insightful art, music, film, and poetry that is already out there, the work that comes from pain, suffering, and brokenness, the work that plumbs the range of human emotion and feeling. Culture in general and the art world in particular is littered with altars to the unknown God (Acts 17) that invite our creative participation. The world desperately needs us to live freely out of the grace that God gives to the Jews in Babylon—to build houses, plant gardens, have families, and seek the welfare of the city (Jer 29:4–9)—to live not as righteous cultural judges, but as broken sinners bearing witness with the arts to God's sustaining grace amidst the city.

But this kind of freedom can happen only if we keep our sinfulness and frailty before us, only if we recognize that what defiles us is not "out there" in the culture, in that painting or that film, but what proceeds from within us (Mark 7:15). God did not call the Jews to Babylon to clean up the city; they are there because of their own disobedience and unrighteousness. It is they, the Jews, who are broken and disobedient. The Babylonians, like the Ninevites in the book of Jonah, "who do not know their right hand from their left" (Jonah 4: 11).

The remembrance of our own unrighteousness and disobedience frees us from the reactionary and defensive posture toward art and culture, allowing us to love our artistic neighbors by loving their art, poetry, music, and film. We are free to make ourselves vulnerable to art, allowing it to work on us *as art* (not as didactic messages, threats to our morality, gauges of cultural health or sickness, or excuses for evangelism). And we are free to mobilize our faith in loving service to that work of art, that painting, that film, that novel, or that poem in order to deepen our understanding of it and to open its depth for others, even (and especially) those who do not share our faith, but whose own lives, not to mention creative work, come from the same places of pain, suffering, and loneliness that ours do.

In this context, the Christian is the ideal audience for all art, for all aesthetic artifacts of the imagination—*even (or especially) the most scandalous and offensive.* It is often the most scandalous and offensive works that reveal the pain, suffering, and desperation of the human condition in the most compelling of ways. And it is the Christian who is free to receive *all things*—including poems and paintings—even those that offend our sensibilities and cause discomfort—as gifts. It is the Christian who can hear the echoes of grace that are often present in them. It is the Christian who sees God at work in the world through artists, writers, and filmmakers who produce artifacts that often contradict their own beliefs, artifacts that strain toward Christ, like trees on a mountain bending toward the warmth of the sun.

Every work of art yearns for a viewer, a reader, a hearer who confesses, "all things were created through him and for him . . . and in him all things hold together" (Col. 1:16–17).

And every painting desires a viewer who receives it not only as creation and gift, but also as promise, a work of art *with a future.*

That is the foundation for Christian witness in culture. And it is the source of our freedom when we experience art.

SPACE

A painting is not its interpretation. At the moment it encounters me in the art museum, a painting exists *for me.* But it does not need me. It exists *for me* in a particular way, a way that challenges my control, rendering me receptive (i.e., passive). T. S. Eliot once said that the meaning of a poem exists somewhere between the poem and the reader. And so it is this "space between" that the painting creates, transforming me, if only briefly, from a subject to an object. It is this moment that Rilke describes in his poem "The Archaic Torso of Apollo" (1908)—the statue confronts and makes a claim on the narrator, whose eye it catches:

> for there is no angle from which
> It does not see you. You must change your life!

The work of art opens up, or perhaps better, reveals the space that exists between the world and me, a space of response and accountability. The work of art roots me out of the pack, shines a spotlight on me, refusing to let me take solace in my human condition, in the collective "us" that displaces individual responsibility. For theologian Gerhard Ebeling, this confrontation, which he calls the "*coram*-relationship," constitutes the existential reality of the human being. We stand before the countenance of the world (*coram mundo*) and before the countenance of God (*coram Deo*).[1] And we do so alone. For Ebeling, following Luther, this reveals the fundamental situation of the human being as one who is on trial—as John Locke observed, *person* is a forensic term.

A work of art activates this *coram* relationship aesthetically, revealing that you and I stand before another—the world, our neighbor, God, and even ourselves—awaiting recognition, judgment, and justification. And what lurks in deep inside us is our failure, our lack—that we bear the mark that the murderer Cain bears. And so Rilke's statue makes a claim on me, demands a response from me.

But I do not want to change my life.

I want to *justify* it—before God, my neighbor, and myself. I want to take charge of the situation, to speak—not be spoken to—to define, to explain, to interpret, to read. I do not want to respond, give account, or receive. Against the Western philosophical tradition, which has followed Aristotle in defining the human being as an active doer—either as a maker or thinker—Martin Luther argued that we are ontologically passive. For Luther a human being is defined—justified—by faith alone (Rom 3: 28).[2] And this passive, receptive posture of faith frees the human being to receive the world as a gift, and to be active in this world through the love of neighbor. "He lives," Luther says, "not in himself, but in Christ and neighbor"[3]—in Christ, passively, through faith and in his neighbor, actively, through love.

My encounter with a painting exposes my ontological passivity, what Luther called the *vita passiva*, in which I stand, as Oswald Bayer says, in the "dative case," that is, in the case of "being given."[4] Yet I fight against it by asserting my control, by behaving as if the painting is a static, inert object, with "subject matter" that needs my interpretive activity to give it life—not an artifact that speaks to me, addresses me, makes me accountable. And so my experience of a painting also reveals my resistance to the receptive life of faith and my addiction to the active life of works, refusing to respect the painting before which I stand as singular event of creative agency that makes a claim on me, reminding me that I am not the subject of my own life story.

1. See Ebeling, *Luther*, 192–209.
2. Luther, "The Disputation Concerning Man," thesis no. 32.
3. Luther, *On Christian Liberty*, 62.
4. Bayer, "The Ethics of Gift," 447.

Luther calls the human person a "rational being with a fabricating heart."[5] The painting before which I stand generates these fabrications—ideas, concepts, frameworks that I create in order to tame it, disenchant it, transform it from something radically other, into something prosaically familiar. Bayer calls this "justifying thinking," which is characterized by "the attempt to mediate and reconcile all things," trying "to fit everything into the concept of the One, the True, the Good, and the Beautiful."[6]

If I can speak of "art" as a theoretical construct, I can avoid the irreducibly particular agency of *that* painting that confronts me at a particular moment, opening up that space that requires the receptive posture of faith to which I must cling that contradicts the urge for explanations, meaning, certainty.

The space that a painting opens up is the space where art criticism dwells. One of the art critic's primary goals is to develop ways to keep that space open in the reader's imagination, to reveal the passivity of the encounter with it while actively responding in such a way that always has the painting, not my interpretive framework, as the subject of the aesthetic sentence. The art critic recognizes that this space is easily foreclosed on by fellow critics, curators, philosophers, and the artists themselves, who recognize the truth in Mark Rothko's claim that it dangerous to send a painting out into the world.

But most importantly, the art critic is aware of his own heart, his own tendency to eliminate that space between himself and the painting, to deflect its claim on him by making it serve his own stories, narratives, projects, and interpretive agenda. And so the art critic must often contradict himself—fight against the urge to suffocate the painting with "meaning," to smooth out its sharp edges. For the art critic, to clear out this space is to make the painting a moving target again, to restore its provocative radicality—its aesthetic sting—as a singular event of a human being's creative agency, which simultaneously achieves its own agency. Or, put another way, the goal of art criticism is to declare the failure of all interpretive schemes to anchor the meaning of a painting, to isolate it only briefly before releasing it back into the wild.

This is an impossible task for me who stands before a painting.

And that is why the space that a painting opens up between the painting and me is a space maintained only by faith working through love (Gal 5:6).

---

5. Quoted in Bayer, *Martin Luther's Theology,* 174.
6. Bayer, *Theology the Lutheran Way,* 26.

A MESSAGE IN A BOTTLE

God calls an artist to be a particular kind of artist in a particular kind of way in the world. This specificity reveals the diversity of artistic practice and the various ways that it is embodied institutionally. Most Christian thinking about art, however, ignores this basic social reality, which every artist (Christian or not) confronts daily. Theological reflection on art does not begin with abstract concepts like "beauty," but in the tall and dangerous grass of the studio, in the anxiety and pressure of the technical and vocational decisions that confront the artist moment by moment.

Whether an artist realizes it or not, every technical decision she makes in her studio proves what kind of artist she is and will be in the world, what kind of witness she will be to art. A work of art is much more and other than a confessional record of the artist's feelings or emotions, or the result of her so-called "creativity" and "innovation." A work of art is an event which unveils a world, and in the process makes a claim on its audience to believe it. In his influential essay, "The American Action Painters" (1950), critic Harold Rosenberg observed, "The lone artist did not want the world to be different, he wanted his canvas to be a world."[7] Made in and through the artist's irreducible individuality, hewn through her experience in and of the world, and wrought in the most private of spaces (her studio), the work of art discloses a world for the world—addressing the inscrutable and irreducible individuality of each viewer when it leaves the studio. And so a work of art is not offered to the world in the abstract or in theory. It is offered literally and concretely to a viewer, one who stands before it, allows herself to be confronted by it, with all of her particular pain and anxiety. To be addressed by it. It is offered *to me*. At that particular moment when I come upon this painting in a gallery or a museum, I am the "world" to whom the artist is offering her world, as it unfolds toward me and my world.

Yet the artist does not know me, does not know the me or the you who will be confronted by the work. In a provocative essay, entitled "To the Addressee," the Russian poet Osip Mandelstam claimed that writing a poem is like putting a message in a bottle and throwing it into the ocean.

> At a critical moment, a seafarer tosses a sealed bottle into the ocean waves, containing his name and a message detailing his fate. Wandering along the dunes many years later, I happen upon it in the sand. I read the message, note the date, the last will and testament of one who has passed on. I have the right to do so. I have not opened someone else's mail. The message in the

7. Rosenberg, "The American Action Painters," 30.

bottle was addressed to its finder. I found it. That means, I have become its secret addressee.[8]

For Mandelstam, the poem finds its audience one person at a time, *through time.*

This is not how we like to think about art or regard anything related to culture, for that matter. We are the ones impatiently in control. We do not want to be addressed beyond the grave, through or across time. I am the one that sees a work of art; I am the one that "interprets" it, vetting its appropriateness according to a list of my own criteria, certainly not drawn from the history and tradition of art that exists outside of me. I am the one that judges a work of art and its "appropriateness." I am active and the work of art is passive. I am the subject and the work of art hanging there on the wall of the museum or gallery is the object of my efforts, my work, my actions. The work awaits *my justification*—my approval or disapproval. And that usually entails its capacity to discern the state of cultural politics, with gauging the score of the culture wars, and an indicator of whether the encroachments of secularism, postmodernism, or whatever bogeyman "isms" have been staved off.

In other words, *we look at art in order to talk about something else, something more important, more relevant, more useful to us.*

But that is simply not why art exists and how it behaves. From an aesthetic point of view, we are passive, receptive, responsive. We listen. The history of criticism is the history of reflection on the relationship—the struggle—between a work of art that exerts itself on the viewer, reader, listener through time, through generations of viewers, readers, listeners. The history of criticism is overflowing with works of art that received condemnation from its contemporaries, but which are now undisputed masterpieces (Melville's *Moby-Dick* is but one of the most glaring). This history is also full of works praised by their audience, which are now forgotten or dismissed as irrelevant at worst, "period pieces" at best. The force that the critic exerts on the work is mitigated by his posture of receptivity, even with work the critic ultimately distrusts, or condemns, or finds problematic. His aggression is a *response* to the activity of the work of art that imposes itself on the critic because he *allows it.* The critic holds her own interpretations loosely, since she must always have Joseph's question before her: "Do not interpretations belong to God" (Gen 40: 8)?

We do not exercise our freedom when we experience a work of art. We are forced to acknowledge the brute fact and infuriating reality that we are not free. We live and breathe and have our being as someone who

8. Mandelstam, "On the Addressee," 68.

has been spoken to, addressed. We have been chosen by that painting. This is a crucial aspect of experiencing art that is ignored by Christians in our rush to "engage" or "transform" culture, and "read" images and creative artifacts alongside the morning paper. We want to apply our "Christian world view," amounting to little more than a list of social conventions, to cultural practices like art, which ask a different approach: a posture of receptivity, humility, and trust that proceeds from the dangerous love of one's neighbor, whether that neighbor is our enemy or a painting.

When I turn a corner in the museum or gallery and, being discovered by a painting, agree to open that message in a bottle, it asks a simple question: "How will *you* respond to *me*?"

That is a question that in our rush to transform, engage, condemn, or otherwise "use" culture for our own purposes, we rarely answer because we rarely hear it since we're often more concerned about the culture "out there" than with our own present encounter with a work of art and the claim it makes on you and me. And by refusing to sit still and listen to what art says, to be the one spoken to, or, in Mandelstam's term, the "addressee," we are deaf to the world that the artist offers us, as a desperate last will and testament.

WHO ARE YOU?

"'Who are *you*?' said the Caterpillar."

—LEWIS CARROLL, *ALICE'S ADVENTURES IN WONDERLAND*

Every painting is a self-portrait. Although he may not be seen on the canvas, the artist is present everywhere. Yet it is a self that even escapes the artist's control, transcending (and sometimes even undermining) his intentions. However, in a self-portrait the artist makes himself present to you and to me, trying to manage how he is perceived. And given the fact that it is the artist's disclosure of himself to his audience, a painted justification of who he is in the world, it is profoundly theological.

The self-portrait makes explicit a fundamental aspect of the human condition—our identity is found before the face of God and before the face of our neighbor. Theologian Gerhard Ebeling observes, "the fundamental situation of man is that of a person on trial . . . and he longs for it as much as he fears it."[9] We exist in the world seeking recognition and justification. A self-portrait actualizes this condition through the relationship of the artist depicting himself directing his gaze at us, confronting us, yet also, somehow, soliciting our recognition.

The German Renaissance artist Albrecht Dürer (1471–1528) and the Dutch Baroque master Rembrandt van Rijn (1606–1669) produced self-portraits that reveal the extremes of self-portraiture as justification in paint.

Painted in 1500 at the height of his artistic powers, Dürer's third and final self-portrait is the first German Renaissance masterpiece. The artist depicts himself within the genre of the holy icon of Christ, as he confronts us directly and his eyes meet our eyes—one of the most important characteristics of the tradition of the Christ icon. The artist's beautiful hair and manicured beard present royal stature, as does the fur that Dürer's right hand fondles (the hand that blesses that is now the hand that paints), displaying his remarkable artistic ability to potential patrons. The artist fills the surface with himself, with his prowess, his authority.[10]

But perhaps the most remarkable presence in the panel is Dürer's famous monogram "AD" and inscription, which function as a claim to copyright, asserting the artist's legal authority over all that comes from his hand (and his head). Despite his identification with Christ, his monogram and inscription on the picture reveal his profound anxiety about his authority as an artist, including his preoccupation with copyright and fear of being plagiarized by inferior artists. And so as we stand judged by Dürer's gaze and awestruck by his artistic authority, we recognize that it is a mask that covers his insecurity, his desperate desire to control and manage his growing reputation and his financial situation as a means of recognition.[11] Although he identifies himself with Christ, Dürer's self-portrait is a legal document presented by a young man on trial to justify his existence, his originality, his value.

A prolific painter of self-portraits, Rembrandt painted over ninety during his lifetime, many because he lacked the financial resources to hire models. Rembrandt was keenly fascinated with the passage of time and representing the nuances and depth of the human personality. The self-portrait painted in 1661, seven years before his death, is entitled *Self-Portrait as the Apostle Paul*. The contrast with Dürer's self-portrait could not be more dramatic. A frail and slightly detached Rembrandt catches our gaze as he turns

9. Ebeling, *Luther*, 197.

10. For the definitive approach to Dürer and self-portraiture, see Koerner, *The Moment of Self-Portraiture in German Renaissance Art*.

11. "Portrait of the artist as an entrepreneur."

away from the Scriptures he is reading. Rembrandt's dark palette and dramatic lighting obscures clothing—the traditional accouterments of power and prestige—to reveal his timeworn and grief-ravaged face. His gaze does not so much confront us as merely concede to our intrusion. Rembrandt identifies with Saint Paul as the "chief of sinners" (1 Tim 1: 15) and one for whom a battle between the old and new Adam wage war within (Rom 7: 24).

Dürer's self-portrait is a powerful mask that hides the anxiety of a young man fighting to control his artistic legacy and financial future, whose anxiety is hidden yet bleeds out as a prominent signature. Dürer will know unspeakable success and receive the praise of kings; yet he will also experience physical suffering and struggle with emotional pain, the latter of which is revealed in his well-known engraving, *Melancholia I*, made fourteen years later.

Rembrandt's self-portrait, on the other hand, is a conscious decision by an old man at the end of his life to give up, remove the mask, and lean into his suffering and weakness. Having earned and lost fortunes, achieved and lost reputation, having known personal heartbreak and professional failure in an emerging art market he could not manage, Rembrandt puts on the mask of St. Paul, one who suffered from a "thorn in the flesh" (2 Cor 12:7) and boasted in his weakness. At the end of his life, Rembrandt depicts himself with nothing but God's promises, the source of his hope, perhaps even as it also represents a rationalization for his failures.

All self-portraits seem to toggle between Dürer's and Rembrandt's. They are masks the artist wears before the world—before his contemporaries and before us (and perhaps before God). If all paintings are, in some sense, self-portraits, then all paintings assert the "artist" before us, whether or not he intends it, and whether or not he can control it. Like these two remarkable self-portraits, all paintings speak of both power and weakness, confidence and anxiety, desperation and detachment, joy and pain.

Yet the eyes of the artist in a self-portrait engage us, recognizing and judging *us*. They ask, as all paintings do: Who are you? What mask do you wear standing here, before me? Before your neighbor, yourself, and God?

ART AND AUDIENCE

A recent article in *Humanities*, entitled "The Image of a Writer," by Randall Fuller, has caused me to give some thought to the audience for a work of art, and how small such an audience is in comparison to more popular arts, feature films, and television programs.[12] An abiding criticism of so-called

12. Fuller, "The Image of a Writer."

"serious" or "fine" art, like poetry and painting, is its elitism—only a small coterie of followers, most of them professor types and intellectuals, seem to care. The audience for a painting or a poem is minuscule compared to the audience for a Hollywood movie, Showtime television series, or viral videos. "Elitism" in this context is simply a way to characterize irrelevance in the face of more obvious forms of power, influence, and value, like box office receipts, Nielsen ratings, or YouTube hits.

Curiously, many Christian thought leaders who take culture seriously tacitly agree with this conclusion. Although they grant them value in theory, they consider poetry and painting to be marginal cultural practices at best because their audiences are so small and thus, by definition, unable to shape or influence culture or the public square, which, in turn, will shape public policy. It is much more effective, the unstated argument goes, to spend our time on those cultural practices and artifacts that attract large audiences than it is to attend to a painting or a poem, especially one made over a century ago, whose reach is not only extremely limited but whose "message" ambiguous at best. There just aren't enough people around a painting or a poem, not enough heads and hearts to form. This situation begs many questions about how cultural influence actually works, questions that James Davison Hunter answers definitively in his book, *To Change the World: The Irony, Tragedy, and Possibility of Christianity in the Late Modern World* (2010).

Most popular cultural artifacts that attract or create a large audience do so for a discrete moment, maximizing its opportunity for its fifteen minutes of fame—the song, television show, or YouTube video that "everyone" seems to be talking about lasts for a very short period. *And then it is completely forgotten.* For many evangelical cultural commentators, it is this moment that attracts their attention. But as quickly as it spikes, so often does it just as quickly disappear from memory. And so Christian thought leaders who claim to be on the cultural cutting edge have an impossible burden to remain fashionable, to chase what's trending. There is certainly a need for cultural commentary in the midst of these white-hot fifteen minutes or seconds, for discerning reflection on where large audiences seem to be emotionally, and how these cultural artifacts, whether top forty singles, television shows, YouTube videos, or the like tap into a collective emotional response to the world.

But what of poems and paintings, those cultural artifacts that never become "popular" in any conceivable sense, that never seem to be at home, to be comfortable at any time? Are these works destined to irrelevance, limited to the seminar room, lecture hall, or cocktail party, entombed in libraries and museums?

Serious art seems to attract an audience differently. While the sitcom or top forty hit is our culture talking to itself, the work of art, whether a poem in an anthology or a painting in a museum, seems to come to us from somewhere else. It speaks *into* our cultural moment from seemingly someplace else. The Spanish philosopher Ortega y Gasset once said that every work of art is contemporary, because we experience it here and now, even though the painting was made by a man in Holland in the eighteenth century or a woman in Taos in the early twentieth. Poems and paintings seem to create or find their audience, slowly, *through time.*

In fact, unlike the sitcom, Hollywood film, or top forty hit, the poems and paintings that are made today seem to be made for another audience. Poems and paintings are not bound to the cultural moment in which they were made. And so the following they accumulate is not limited to the historical, social, or cultural moment into which they were born. In fact, some works, like Dickinson's poems or Melville's *Moby-Dick*, the two examples Fuller discusses, were oddly destined for a reader, for an audience, *only in the future.*

Russian poet Osip Mandelstam's comparison of poetry to writing a last will and testament and putting it in a bottle, sealing it, and tossing it into the ocean is apt. Whoever discovers that bottle many years later, long after the death of writer, and reads that message, is the one who was intended to be addressed.

Poetry and painting seem to find their audience in the future. The best ones do so generation after generation, century after century, creating and then accumulating an audience that can far exceed any audience that a "viral" cultural artifact could achieve. Moreover, the poem or painting is never truly forgotten. It always remains to be rediscovered by a critic, either in museum storage or in the library stacks. In fact, Fuller suggests,

> Ultimately, if paradoxically, it was Dickinson and Melville's refusal to court and attain a mass audience while they lived that has resulted in their enduring canonical status. Early in the twentieth century, both artists were "rediscovered" and appropriated by scholars and cultural opinion-makers.[13]

The "enduring canonical status" of a Dickinson or a Melville occurs because what is often heard in a work of art unfolds over time, needing the time of subsequent works of art, of poems and paintings that allow previously unheard works to be heard without the chatter of the artist's own milieu. The canon evolves only in time, through history, and is always retrospective. The

13. Ibid.

role of the critic is to give to a work of art what it most desperately needs, that is, time to be heard by someone in the future.

That this other kind of audience for cultural artifacts, an audience that exists over time, as the artifact survives you and me, should caution in two ways. First, it should warn us against absolutizing our present cultural moment, seeing in it either the best or the worst. (It is important also in this context to keep in mind that we live "between the times," that is, between Christ's first and second coming, a time of conflict and a time in which "culture" is becoming neither categorically "better" nor "worse," and that God is busy at work whether we think this is the best of times or the worst of times.) Second, we must be less certain about what amounts to cultural influence. J. G. Hamann reminds us that we stitch on the underside of the carpet—we do not have the privilege of seeing God's handiwork as he weaves the beautiful tapestry. One of the unique roles of the art critic at this cultural moment is to maintain space for God's work to be done in and through such unexpected artifacts as a poem or a painting. Moreover, as Christian Wiman has written, "People who think poetry has no power have a very limited conception of what power means."[14] And they have a very limited conception of the kinds of work that God uses to be busy and active in this world. We privilege the best seller or the election, worship those with massive Twitter followings. Compared to *Breaking Bad* or *Mad Men*, a poem by Emily Dickinson or a painting by Edvard Munch seems weak and ineffectual. Yet God chose the foolish things of the world to humble the wise (1 Cor 1:27).

Poems and paintings remind us of the audience to come, remind us that we are not the final destination, but become part of a community of listeners that transcend time and space, nationality, and custom. Poems and paintings remind us not only that the work of a poet's or painter's hands have a future, but that the work of ours do as well (Ps 90: 17). If we are unsure about how God can use something like a poem or a painting, that doubt derives in large part from the insecurity and doubt we feel about the influence of our own work. Like a poem or a painting, we cannot know the audience for our work, the impact that our work has not only in the present, but also in the future.

Poems and paintings that have succeeded in accruing an audience through time have done so because there were contemporary readers and viewers who sensed the significance of the work as a manifestation of some aspect of human experience and labored diligently to reveal it, most often in the face of ridicule or apathy, with the belief that this poem or that painting

14. Wiman, *My Bright Abyss*, 114.

was worth passing on to the future. These sensitive and prescient supporters believed that even though this painter or that poet had not found their audience yet, they would in the future. The responsibility of this reader, of that viewer, was to make sure those poems and paintings reached their destined audience, buying them time, as it were. Is it possible to conceive of poems and paintings that have transcended the moment of their making as eschatological, as somehow a foretaste of a future hope, as human work that has faith in a future?

We would do well to attend to this eschatological aspiration that characterizes poems and paintings, that the audience of a work of art is never exclusively in the present, and so its justification is found elsewhere, usually in the future. Fuller's essay reveals once again that poems and paintings— so-called "serious" art—are weak and vulnerable things. They need help to survive the present in order to find their audience in the future. Where are those poems and paintings that are being made today that reveal that eschatological yearning? How can we help them?

Are we too busy following the crowds to notice this artist or that poet, whose work seems strangely out of joint with the times? And if we do find this artist or that poet, this poem or that painting, are we willing to use our cultural influence simply and merely to insure its future, to give it space and time to enable it to find its audience in the future?

Poems and paintings remind us that we are eschatological creatures. We live in faith entirely from what God has promised us, "that our only true being is the self that we will become."[15] They are reminders that "the world is kept for God's future."[16] And that alone makes it worth our effort to cultivate them, and worth our effort to pass them on to an audience in the future, for indeed, poems and paintings exist in part because of their maker's faith in the future.

---

15. Iwand, *The Righteousness of Faith According to Luther*, 78–79.
16. Bayer, *Freedom in Response*, 238.

3

THE ART WORLD

In the space between hearing and speaking, being judged and judging, we find ourselves in this world not in some harmony that has already been achieved, but in the midst of a battle of controversies and conflicting interpretations.

—OSWALD BAYER

Every creature will simultaneously become your sacrifice and your idol.

—J. G. HAMANN

Your life shall hang in doubt before you. Night and day you shall be in dread and have no assurance of your life.

—DEUTERONOMY 28:66

ART AFTER THE FIFTH GRADE

There are few cultural practices more misunderstood and misinterpreted than art. It starts in grade school art classes and is affirmed every step of the way through adulthood. We are taught that art is fun; it is whatever you want it to be; anyone can do it if they really want to; and that it expresses your individuality and creativity. What is more, we also learn that professional artists are quirky creative types that don't quite "fit in" with the rest of us. We are also taught that art is nice decoration to have around and it is important somehow for our local communities, but thoroughly unnecessary for daily life. We are told that even though we don't know much about art, we know good art when we see it. The church contributes simply by adding a layer of theological justification to these presumptions and the claim that the art world needs to be transformed, redeemed, or otherwise made safe for the "Christian artist."

But then we read in the newspapers about a controversial artist in London, for example, who uses dead animals, like a shark, and puts them in tanks of formaldehyde, calls them art, and is celebrated as one of the great artists of our generation by scholars with PhDs who write long, impenetrable essays in journals few people read. More perplexing still, someone pays twelve million dollars for artwork, and then lends it the Metropolitan Museum of Art.

Let the World Be the World

What are we as Christians to make of this discrepancy between the messages and training we receive as children and what occurs in London, New York, Berlin, and Paris; about what we think is art and what the professionals claim? How are we to respond?

As Christians we stand *coram Deo* (before God) in faith, passively, so that we can stand *coram mundo* (before the world), actively in love. We are free, as Gerhard Ebeling writes,

> To let the world be the world—not with the undertone of weary resignation which we usually give to that phrase, but in the sense of taking responsibility for the world, having proper dealings with the world, doing justice to it, i.e., giving it its due.[1]

To give the art world its due, to do it justice, is to first and foremost seek to understand it, to discover how and in what way it values a stuffed shark as

1. Ebeling, *Word and Faith*, 403–4.

art (Damien Hirst), and to do so on its own terms. We must resist the temptation to fall back upon our romanticized assumptions of what we've learned since childhood, which obscures the fact that "art" consists of numerous different and even overlapping "art worlds"—that is, complex institutional frameworks of production and distribution that are essential to the meaning and significance of the work produced in and for them. To interpret Hirst's stuffed shark within the framework in which we've been trained in fifth-grade craft classes and community arts programs—that is, to complain that it is obscure and does not rely on the "talent" of the artist—is to be unjust not only to the stuffed shark but to the art world for which it was intended and to which it is a response. Art is one of the few cultural practices that seems from the outside not to require significant work, practice, or training to understand. But like all cultural practices, art requires practice and initiation. A middle school education seems adequate to recognize, appreciate, and judge it—perhaps even to make it. The problem, however, is that we use our fifth-grade craft classes as the standard to judge all art, including the art that is made for a very different audience (not a *better* audience, I must stress, but a *different* one).

The contemporary art world is our neighbor that we are called and freed to love. And loving it means working hard to understand how it works, discovering how its institutional structures and frameworks confer meaning and value, and entering into a creative conversation with its participants.

An Exotic Tribe

A good place to start is Sarah Thornton's acclaimed book, *Seven Days in the Art World,* which offers the curious reader an insider's perspective on our strange and mysterious neighborhood, which values a twelve-million dollar stuffed shark and venerates other works of art that don't fit our preconceptions about what art should look like. Thornton reveals a very different world of art than most of us are used to. And that is a very good thing. Her book is the result of several years of sociological and ethnographical field research among the mysterious and exotic tribe that comprises the international art world, learning its language and observing and interpreting its behavior. It is organized around seven high-profile art world traditions that shine a spotlight, in different ways, on the key social roles in this particular art world: the artist, dealer, critic, curator, collector, and auction house expert.

Thornton argues that art is not merely about a particular kind of object or artifact but about social roles, behaviors, means of distribution, and beliefs that make something called "art" possible and through which certain objects and artifacts are experienced and interpreted as meaningful. This sociological approach to art has been given considerable attention by such writers as Jean Duvignaud, Arthur Danto, George Dickie, and Nicholas Wolterstorff, among others.[2] In this context, art is not a qualitative judgment but a particular cultural practice that acquires meaning and significance within a specific institutional framework, which generates a living tradition that guides and provokes artistic decisions, to which artists respond and pass on, and which audiences likewise must learn.

Thornton's narrative revolves around two major themes. Her first, which she reiterates time and again throughout her account, is that "great works do not just arise, they are made—not just by artists and their assistants but also by the dealers, curators, critics, and collectors who 'support' the work."[3] The art world works to give value to the work of art. And second, she argues that the art world is a secular religion. The contemporary art world, Thornton suggests, "is a loose network of overlapping subcultures held together by a belief in art." Thornton continues, "It demands leaps of faith, but it rewards the believer with a sense of consequence."[4] It is not a homogeneous or monolithic institution; it consists of a matrix of communities and institutions that are animated by what Thornton calls "a kind of alternative religion for atheists." Belief holds this peculiar art world together, and belief is mediated through a tradition.

Thornton's first chapter follows the drama of a public auction at a November sale at Christie's in New York through the eyes of the auction house's chief auctioneer, Christopher Burge. Thornton then moves to the other coast to sit in on one of artist Michael Asher's famous twenty-four-hour "crits," a distinctive educational event (or, rather, performance) at Cal Arts, one of the nation's top art schools, in which a group of students explores each member's work. Thornton then devotes the third chapter to an analysis of the famous summer art fair Art Basel in Switzerland, where, not surprisingly, she runs into many of the same dealers, collectors, artists, and auction house specialists she had met in New York. In contrast to the tightly run and orchestrated sales at Christie's, the art fair in Basel is a chaotic gathering of dealers from around the world. The strange relationship between collectors and dealers is Thornton's topic, as each jostles for business leverage through the value or perceived value of the art on view. The collectors play the role

2. Duvignaud, *The Sociology of Art*; Dickie, *The Art Circle*; Arthur Danto, "The Artworld"; Nicholas Wolterstorff, *Art in Action*.

3. Thornton, *Seven Days in the Art World*, xiv.

4. Ibid.

of the coquette, attracting the attention of dealers and playing them off each other.

Thornton then redirects her focus to the artist through an examination of the Turner Prize, the world's best-known contemporary art competition, sponsored by the Tate Gallery in London and presided over by the Tate Modern's venerable director, Sir Nicholas Serota, along with a four-member jury. The winner of the prize has often been controversial, including Damien Hirst in 1995. Thornton then explores the role of the critic in her chapter entitled "The Magazine," in which she travels to New York to spend time with Tim Griffin, chief editor, and his colleagues from *Artforum*, the world's most respected art magazine. Thornton reveals how seriously the critics associated with the magazine take their roles as interpreters and evaluators of contemporary art. She then travels to Tokyo to visit the studio of Japanese superstar artist Takashi Murakami as the artist prepares for his major retrospective exhibition at the Museum of Contemporary Art (MOCA) in Los Angeles. Thornton reveals an artist who is a far cry from the romantic bohemian slacker, making art in isolation and largely unaware of such bourgeois concerns as "business." Rather, Murakami shrewdly presides over a large and complex corporation with dozens of employees. Thornton concludes her narrative with the Venice Biennale, the world's oldest and most famous international exhibition, in which participating nations present their own exhibitions in special pavilions built by each nation. Thornton profiles the former MoMA curator and current dean of the Yale School of Art, Robert Storr, who was the first American-born curator to assume the position of director of the Biennale. Because her account documents the art world at its height, only a few years before the Wall Street crash of October 2008 burst its bubble, Thornton ends her book with a reflection on the implications of the new conditions that now prevail in this art world, and her continued fascination with it.

A Response

For those Christians who might think that Thornton's *Seven Days* chronicle degrades or compromises the purity of art and its meaning because she appreciates the social structures of the art world and addresses the brute fact that art is a business and big business: it's time to grow up. Seduced by nostalgia for the innocence of our fifth-grade art classes, distraught that the church is no longer its primary patron, and armed with a theological aesthetics that idealizes and dumbs down "beauty," we Christians who want to care about art (in theory) are often bitterly disappointed by the art world (in practice). But that is not the art world's problem; it is ours.

Serious art in the Western tradition—that is, art that is not content to "image" what we think we already know about the world of appearances and experiences, but probes more deeply into the nature of such reality through aesthetic form—has always been inextricably bound up with business. It is inseparable from patrons and collectors, with markets and dealers, with personalities and egos. It is indistinguishable from all of those aspects that are so easily dismissed by contemporary Christian critics as an alien infestation of modernity, but has been with art all along, present even when the church was its primary, if not exclusive, patron.

Great art emerges out of the warp and woof—some might say the muck and mire—of commerce, of production and distribution that is at the very heart of *Seven Days in the Art World*. Can it be any other way? Lives devoted to Christ emerge out of the warp and woof—muck and mire—of nasty church council meetings, contentious denominational conventions, personality conflicts, budget cuts and fund-raising, and fights over who's serving the coffee after the service. This is where and how we must live out our vocations, inside and outside the church, east of Eden, after the fall. And this is how those who participate in this art world must live out their professional callings. Art can often seduce us into idealizations that unconsciously deny the reality of the fall as we talk about beauty and creativity as if they are abstractions that simply float harmlessly above the messiness of daily life.

The contemporary art world, with all the fascinating and irritating mechanizations that Thornton chronicles, deserves a robust and thick sociological analysis from a Christian perspective, that we live "between the times," in the "already" and "not yet" of the old and new world. It is a perspective that can distinguish between God and the world, allowing the world to be the world, in all of its brokenness. This means that there is no hand-wringing or condemnation because such a structure fails to conform to our fifth-grade ideals. We cannot fail to recognize that this art world that Thornton describes does not operate outside God's active presence in the world and our responsibility is to serve it, by loving it, and that begins by seeking to understand it.

Throughout her account, Thornton observes that this art world functions as a religion for many of the participants. This should interest us, for it makes clear that the stakes in the art world are existentially high and therefore inherently theological: the institution of art is the means by which many of its participants bring order into their lives, justifying their very existence to another—the world, themselves, or God.

Thornton's observation that the contemporary art world requires faith opens up productive space for Christian reflection on contemporary art that addresses the complex, convoluted, and opaque frameworks and structures that institutionalize the human need for justification by faith. Yet, despite the fact that the art world generates such aesthetic self-justifications (idols), it also produces works of art that incomprehensibly, inexplicably point toward an alien presence in the world, a hint, a faint echo, a sweet aroma from beyond the hills that testifies to God's promises that there is a "deeper magic" (C. S. Lewis), a day after (Victor Hugo), and that all will be well (Julian of Norwich). As a result, the contemporary art world is littered with altars to the Unknown God (Acts 17). Our responsibility as Christians is to roll up our sleeves and engage this world that Thornton presents by *listening* to it, rather than judging it self-righteously according to some romantic misconceptions that presuppose that it needs to be transformed to reflect our own idolatries. We must instead creatively and imaginatively engage and name those altars as a means to preach the justifying grace of Christ at work in the world—even in a part of that world in which a stuffed shark is art.

THE SCREAM, A STUFFED SHARK, AND THE INSECURITY OF CULTURE

There appears to be a disparity between the record sale at auction of Edvard Munch's *The Scream* (1895) as confirmation of Munch's canonical status in the history of modern art and the artist's profound anxiety and fear that led to the production of the picture. The auction is the nerve center of the contemporary art world, where the collective aspirations and fears of artists, collectors, dealers, and other art professionals find expression in the highly orchestrated gestures of the auction house. It is the primary site in the art world in which men and women participate in what Hegel called a life-or-death battle for mutual recognition. As such, it is one of the most profoundly theological locations in contemporary culture, where the ultimate value of life, a person's justification, is at stake with each lot and with each bid.

The media recognizes the disparity and the strangeness of the auction house, yet overlooks its life-or-death consequences. Commentators interpret the outrageous prices for oil paint smeared on scraps of canvas to be a sham at the worst or, at best, merely a playground for the too wealthy and too bored. But it is precisely in its outrageously out-of-touch expressions at auction that the art world itself raises the most profound theological questions,

questions that implicate and describe every human being, including you and me.

The Market

The British artist Damien Hirst is often brought forth as Exhibit A for the outrageous irrelevance of the art world and its bizarre market mechanizations. In 2012, Hirst presented over three hundred "spot" paintings at dealer Larry Gagosian's eleven galleries around the world (most of them painted by his assistants).[5] Several years earlier, Hirst even produced an exhibition that he presented, with no precedent, directly at auction.[6] But it is Hirst's installation, *The Physical Impossibility of Death in the Mind of Someone Living* (1991), which has become the icon of the irrelevance of the art world. Commissioned by the British advertising executive and art collector Charles Saatchi, the fourteen-foot stuffed tiger shark suspended in a tank filled with formaldehyde was sold in 2005 to the American hedge fund executive Stephen Cohen for $12 million and then placed on loan to the Metropolitan Museum of Art. This work embodies, like no other, the mysterious opacity and alleged disconnect of the contemporary art world, a source of either derision or frustration for all except those who live in this bubble of luxurious overindulgence and irresponsibility.

Yet the art world is much more than meets the eye. It is not a playground for the rich, but a battlefield, a war zone in which human value through recognition is conferred or withheld, where emotional lives hang in the balance. With its holy days, liturgies, relics, and other practices that create and maintain belief, the art world operates like a religion, conferring ontological significance and justification to the lives of the participants through the currency of artifacts like Hirst's spot paintings and stuffed sharks. But it is a religion that demands sacrifice. As J.G. Hamann poignantly and powerfully observed, "Every creature will alternately become your sacrifice and your idol."[7]

Economist Don Thompson has explored this darker and subrational side of the art world in *The $12 Million Stuffed Shark: The Curious Economics of Contemporary Art* (2008). The book analyzes the mystifying economic structure that characterizes contemporary art at the highest echelons. For Thompson, this art world is defined by insecurity. "Never underestimate," states an auction house director, "how insecure buyers are about

5. Smith, "Hirst, Globally Dotting His 'I.'"
6. Vogel, "Damien Hirst's Next Sensation—Thinking Outside the Dealer."
7. Quoted in Bayer, *A Contemporary in Dissent*, 82.

contemporary art, and how much they always need reassurance."[8] Insecurity is the fuel that powers the network of auction houses, galleries, museums, and scholarly interpretation, each of which serves as different validating mechanisms, reinforcing decisions to acquire, represent, exhibit, or review an artist's work. Thompson's book suggests that this rarely has to do with the quality of the work of art itself, but leverage of secondary indicators. "The value of art often has more to do with artist, dealer, or auction-house branding, and with collector ego, than it does with art."[9] But the collector's ego is fragile. "Most of all," Thompson writes, "they want reassurance that, when they hang the art, their friends will not ridicule their purchase."[10] Whether it is $12 million for a stuffed shark or $200,000 for a canvas with oil paints smeared on it, collectors need to be confident that their purchase brings power, prestige, and cultural capital. They are desperate to alleviate the doubt that hangs before them (Deut 28:66).

Artists who work at this level and in this particular context of the art world know this deep angst and doubt that pervades dealers and collectors and they develop their own strategies to provide such reassurance. "The job of the artist," Francis Bacon once said, "is always to deepen the mystery." It is the mystery, the great cloud of unknowing, that can alleviate (although it never completely eliminates) the doubt. The strange personas and outrageous gestures of Andy Warhol, Joseph Beuys, Damien Hirst, Jeff Koons, and Maurizio Cattelan are intentionally crafted efforts to enchant collectors, easing their insecurity. In an age when collectors and dealers regularly consult a website called Artfacts (www.artfacts.net), which tracks artists like stocks, their worth rising and falling on a daily basis, such strategies are important means by which artists preserve their creative autonomy and artistic integrity in the midst of the battlefield disguised as a cocktail reception.

The insecurity that haunts collectors and dealers can crush artists, forcing them into a high-stakes game of behavioral poker, in which their very livelihoods and identities are determined by a small group of wealthy but unpredictable collectors fueled by a powerful and unpredictable cocktail of indulgent entertainment and desperate validation. To dismiss this as antithetical to the integrity of art overidealizes it and distorts the social and institutional fabric from which art emerges. Moreover, this situation is the same for a painter of landscapes as it is for Damien Hirst. It was also the same for an artist like Munch, whose decision to leave Germany and return

8. Thompson, *The $12 Million Stuffed Shark*, 9.

9. Ibid., 228.

10. Ibid., 118.

to his native Norway was a strategic effort to diversify the market for his work before the outbreak of World War I.[11]

East of Eden

The "curious economics of contemporary art" that Thompson explores is a distinctive manifestation of the all-too-human struggle for mutual recognition, for the justification of our very existence. Like the builders of the Tower of Babel, art becomes a means by which we "make a name for ourselves" (Gen 11:4), and that name is a matter of life or death. For one's existential fate, in the words of Hegel, demands that "they recognize themselves as mutually recognizing one another."[12] Those institutions that make up the art world—the auction houses, museums, galleries, and the like—are means by which human beings find and maintain that recognition that justifies their existence. And a reason why the prices for many works of art are so exorbitant is because a price tag cannot be placed on one's justification. In addition, like Naaman offering immense wealth to Elijah in response to the latter cleansing the former's leprosy (2 Kgs 5), it is often through wealth and power that the world responds to the recognition that something profoundly theological is at stake, something that bears on their very right to exist.

The overwhelming anxiety that is not only at the heart of the contemporary art world but characterizes all cultural practices can only be relieved through the reception of the world (nature and culture) as "creation," as God's good gift to the human person and the response to make and to name (Gen 2:19). Yet it must also be acknowledged that such work is now done east of Eden, the entrance of which remains guarded (Gen 3:24), and is now done in the shadow of and intertwined with toil, pain, insecurity, and death. And it is also done as a way to make a name for ourselves, to use our work, our creativity and imagination, to solicit justification from God and the world. Therefore, all cultural endeavors, including art, emerge from suffering, pain, and fear as often as joy, from pride as well as gratitude.

Great works of art can articulate both the experience of crushing, suffocating alienation as well as the effect of the life-giving freedom of grace, a beautiful defiance of death and promise of life that finds its origin in Christ's comforting words, "I am with you always, to the end of the age" (Matt 28:20). Yet the remarkable experiences that a work of art can produce in the viewer occurs not in some isolated laboratory or seminar room, but in the

---

11. Prelinger, *After the Scream*, 46–55.
12. Quoted in Bayer, *Freedom in Response*, 24.

art world, whose perfect embodiment is the cutthroat high-stakes game of the auction.

Perhaps there is, after all, not such a wide disparity between the desperation of the man who painted *The Scream* in 1895, and the man who outbid his rivals for it in 2012.

DEATH, WINE, AND CHEESE

The artist exists in awkward relationship to her audience. She labors for many months, perhaps several years, to produce an exhibition of paintings to present to the public. She sacrifices time with her family and friends, isolating herself emotionally, intellectually, and physically. She reads, thinks, writes, reflects on her work, often questioning, doubting, and, on more than one occasion, vowing to cancel the show altogether.

In other words, our artist experiences death—she dies to others, perhaps, but it is to herself that she truly dies. The meaning of her life becomes inextricably interwoven with those paintings that cannot be finished as the exhibition looms on the calendar. Perhaps she invites a handful of people into her studio to see the work in progress—her boyfriend, a close friend, a critic, the curator, or a trusted collector. She gauges their reaction—what they say, what they don't say. She imagines how viewers will respond to the gesture from that figure, the color of that tree, the look on that little girl's face.

Our artist lives with doubt and fear. Success in the studio yesterday is completely forgotten when she is confronted with the results the next morning. She begins to understand what Cézanne meant when he said somewhere, "with every stroke, I risk my life."

And so it goes for weeks and months.

It is often said that artists suffer from a post-exhibition crisis—after they complete a body of work and present it in an exhibition, they go through a period of mourning. And from my experience this is so. They have changed. Something in them has died in order for something else to live.

At the opening of the exhibition, our artist appears, dressed not for the studio but for a performance. She makes herself pretty. (She has told her boyfriend to stay home.) She shakes hands and kisses cheeks, nibbles on some cheese. Perhaps drinks a glass of wine—but only one. She accepts the congratulations and tries to smile a lot and laugh. She's asked about the paintings. And she makes up some explanations. (She's rehearsed several lines that will satisfy her listeners and prevent her from having to talk more about the paintings.)

She's not interested in talking about her work. In fact, it revolts her. As she engages in mindless banter and witty small talk, gets flirted with relentlessly, she watches how people respond to this or that painting, how long they linger in front of them. She feels exposed *and* invisible. She realizes, much to her surprise, that she is not the same person who painted those pictures, although she is not quite sure yet who she has become.

She observes her audience, those who are drifting in and out, chatting with friends and strangers, laughing and catching up on family and career, drinking wine, hovering over the elaborate spread. She notices that they rarely look at the paintings. And she reminds herself they are here for one particular reason.

They've had a hard day at work and they want to relax—relax with a glass of wine, a bit of nosh, and some culture—in that order. They have told their friends to meet them at the gallery opening. And then it's on to dinner. The paintings are part of the process of unwinding, of softening the hard edges created by a difficult and stressful day at the office. The gallery becomes a place to decompress and recharge for an evening out with spouse, partner, or friends—or perhaps a nice buffer between work and more business over dinner with clients. An exhibition of paintings offers an attractive backdrop for such social commerce.

She remembers a few months ago, sitting in front of her paintings in her studio, thinking about how they would be heard and who would hear them. She remembers not imagining her audience balancing a drink and dish or having a business conversation in front of them.

She imagined someone else. She imagined someone who needed them as desperately as she needed to paint them.

Yet those at the opening reception, distracted by the workday and looking forward to the evening's events, are the ones who must buy the paintings in order for our artist to make rent, keep the lights on in her studio, and pay her child's tuition bill that's due in two weeks. Through her work in the studio that has resulted in these paintings, she has died countless times, forced to relinquish power and control, abandon presuppositions and presumptions about her work, what it communicates about who she is and her relationship to the world. And her paintings, like all authentic works of art, beckon the viewer to die as well.

Yet her livelihood depends on gaining the favor of those who regard art to be a form of relaxation, entertainment, leisure—those for whom art and other signs of "culture" serve to deny death and achieve recognition. Her career depends on those who collect art because they like being around "creativity" and "beauty," aspire to become cultured, and enjoy the new social networks and opportunities that being an art collector offers.

And our artist knows this. She knows that there are two collectors who care about her work, who talk to her about how it kills them, has transformed them, how they have learned about themselves and the world through her paintings. (They've even had some conversations about God.) Yet these collectors are the exception. (And they came by the gallery before the opening to congratulate her, put a hold on two of her works, and have, by now, disappeared.) They cannot pay *all* her bills. She needs the others, the ones for whom painting is entertainment, speculation, and investment. And that is why her dealer is flitting about the exhibition space talking to them, pulling her into inane conversations about the slopes in Aspen or if she knows so-and-so in Palm Beach, or whether she'll be at Art Basel this summer. But what she really wants to talk about is suffering. And whether art can teach anyone anything.

She recalls that the Russian poet Osip Mandelstam compared writing a poem to putting a note in a bottle and throwing it out to sea. The person who happens upon it, washed up on the beach, is the one for whom the poem is addressed.

Our artist will be invited to a large dinner hosted by her dealer to celebrate her exhibition. She'll be seated next to the collectors that her dealer wants her to get to know. She doesn't want to go. She wants to go home and cry. But she will go. She will listen to the collectors talk about their art collections, their furniture in Santa Fe, that wild night with this or that artist in Paris or Berlin. She'll try to keep up with the laughing. She'll make eye contact with the men and look pretty and talk to their wives about motherhood and schools.

All the collectors at the dinner express serious interest in her paintings. One of the spouses will complain about the colors or the size of the pictures being too big for their guest bedroom, another will wish her work was "less serious." (In the end, only two of the collectors will buy paintings. One will pay immediately. The other will take months to pay. But she will make rent and pay off her child's tuition for the semester.)

She'll go home.

And she'll think about why those paintings that she risked so much on exist in the world.

And for whom?

VOCATION AND THE ARTIST'S STUDIO

In February 2013 I was in Pittsburgh to speak on modern art and grace at the annual Jubilee Conference, an event that brings 2,000 college students together to connect their faith to their work. After my presentation, a person working in campus ministry asked how he could support two students who happen to be artists. His question revealed just how art can challenge assumptions about vocational discipleship and the theology of work in the church.

The vocation conversation, which has emerged with new vigor in the church, ranges from work-life balance, to the pressures of ministry, to what vocations are "off-limits" for Christians, to workplace ethics, maximizing efficiency and productivity, and leadership development.[13] This conversation about calling and work is underwritten theologically by the "cultural mandate" of Genesis 1:28 and our role in the eschatological fulfillment of the kingdom, whether in transforming, redeeming, making, or bearing witness to and being a faithful presence in culture.[14]

Usually absent from these conversations is the work of the artist. When the artist does figure into discussions about vocation, she is often romanticized to the margins. Either she is described as the mysterious producer of a theological abstraction, "beauty," or is reduced to an outside-the-box vision caster whose "creativity" adds value or a little seasoning to this or that organization or project. This problem is not limited to the church. It's a cultural problem, for we are skeptical of art's usefulness. However, I would like to suggest that artists offer an important voice in the vocational conversation, which we can see if we go inside the artist's studio.

Midlife Crisis at Nineteen

Art students face crucial vocational questions of value that usually confront others only later in their careers. The questions that a forty-five year old lawyer asks, like "what am I doing this for?," are usually asked by the art student her first semester in college, when she has to justify to her parents why they should pay hundreds of dollars per credit hour for her to push paint around on a canvas, with little in the way of stable job prospects after graduation. And for her entire career as an artist, she will struggle with the value of spending long hours in the studio producing paintings that undermine our

13. See Keller and Alsdorf, *Every Good Endeavor*; Sherman, *Kingdom Calling*; Ballor, *Get Your Hands Dirty*; and Veith, *God at Work*.

14. Mouw, *When the Kings Come Marching In*.

culture's presumptions, inside and outside the church, about the use, value, and relevance of her work. And she'll struggle with finding a part-time or full-time job that will allow her time and energy to work in the studio.

Who is an Artist?

There are few cultural practices with a less clearly demarcated professional structure than art. There is no equivalent to the bar exam, no board that confers the title "artist" on a person. Moreover, we are trained since grade school to regard art as something everyone can do, if they want to. And so the art student, from the very beginning, must struggle with recognition and justification in an especially acute way. What makes me an artist? Does my neighbor recognize me as an artist? Educational credentials, which usually mean so much in the workforce, are not helpful in establishing a difference between one who has an MFA from an Ivy League school and says, "I'm an artist," and another who is an investment banker and takes up painting to relax, who likewise claims, "I'm an artist." The artist's vocational identity, then, must have a countercultural perspective, one that can underwrite its value in the face of its precarious status among the professions, which contradicts conventional definitions of success.

Stereotypes

The myth of the tortured artist—which has a long and distinguished history—who feels more deeply, struggles with depression, addiction, and alienation, is often used to put the artist "over there," away from "us," either on a pedestal or in the gutter. But that posture overlooks one very important reality: the artist is *exactly* like us. Art, as Edvard Munch reminds us, comes from pain. And if we're honest with ourselves, we have to admit that most of our work comes from pain, the struggle for recognition, and the desire to close a wound that has remained open our entire lives. We struggle with the same existential problems and insecurities as Munch. We worry that our work, at the end of the day (or at the end of our lives), will mean nothing, will not matter. Yet our professions usually insulate us from confronting these questions as directly and powerfully as an artist does each time she goes into her studio to work, and brings with her doubt, fear, and struggles—precisely the emotions that most of our professions have trained us to leave somewhere else, either at home or at the bar down the street.

More than a Paycheck

The discussion of vocation inside the evangelical community and beyond often limits itself to career choice and placement. Yet for Martin Luther, vocation was much more comprehensive. It was the result of reflection on the social implications of the doctrine of justification, forming how we respond to the faith that the Word has created that frees us to love our neighbor. For Luther, our vocation, the work that we do, is neither for our own fulfillment nor for God's approval. *It is for our neighbor.* And the doctrine of vocation underwrites all of our social roles, not just the one at the office, the one for which we went to college and grad school. From the outset, art students must recognize that their calling as artists consists of more than a pursuit of a respectable professional identity, comfortable living, and the capacity to acquire stuff. They will produce works for an audience (neighbor) they may never know. Moreover, most art students come to understand that they will not make a living as artists. This is the case for nearly all artists, even those who are "successful." Many must supplement their income creatively through teaching, real estate, or other endeavors that offer the financial stability to pursue their vocations as artists without the pressure of selling their work in order to pay the bills.

Vocation, the Artist's Studio, and a Theology of the Cross

It is this gap between work and paycheck that offers a productive space for further theological reflection on vocation in the artist's studio, especially reflection that takes seriously failure, suffering, and doubt. Too often discussions of vocation in the church are held captive by an obsession with creating narratives of power and success, which hide the constant presence of fear, failure, and doubt. These "theologies of glory," as Luther calls them, preserve the human capacity to please God through good works. In contrast, Luther offered a "theology of the cross," which, beginning with the humiliation of the cross, privileging the foolish things that shame the wise (1 Cor 1:27), finds God present in and working with and through suffering, failure, and pain.

The history of art reveals the artist's studio to be a place where suffering, failure, doubt, and pain are confronted, lived with, and through which meaningful work often emerges. Far from being irrelevant to the conversation on vocation, an exception that proves the rule, the artist's studio connects with the universal human anxiety about the meaningfulness and value of their work, producing the manic response of exaggerated importance as well as debilitating despair. Whether or not we understand art or the artistic process, the challenges and decisions that face an artist, even an art student on a college campus, are ones with which we can identify and, in fact, help us consider a doctrine of vocation that is cross-shaped.

THE CITY, THE COUNTRY, AND THE ARTIST

Cities have attracted artists, musicians, and writers for centuries. Patronage, an educated audience that values the arts, and, perhaps most important, a robust community of creative peers to encourage and challenge artistic practice, have made cities fundamental to the history of art.

However, the artists and writers I've been thinking about recently have, at crucial moments in their careers, left dynamic urban centers for the country. Herman Melville left Manhattan in 1850 for a 160-acre farm in Pittsfield, Massachusetts, to write his masterpiece *Moby-Dick*. Norwegian painter Edvard Munch left Berlin and its fertile bohemian avant-garde community in 1909 for a solitary, rural life in his native Norway; Abstract Expressionist Jackson Pollock left New York City in the late 1940s for the rural setting of The Springs, Long Island, followed by friend Willem de Kooning in the late '50s. And many more—Henry David Thoreau, Robert Frost, Robinson Jeffers, Anselm Kiefer—have left the city to do their most important work.

In 2012 my friend, artist Makoto Fujimura, joined this list. After many years of working in and for New York City as an artist and creative catalyst, he moved his home and studio to an old farmhouse outside of Princeton, New Jersey, which he has come to call Fuji Farm.

Because they deal in and work with the ineffable, ephemeral, and transitory states of experiences and feelings, artists are particularly shaped and affected by their environment. How has riding the subway numerous times each day over the last decade shaped Fujimura's thought patterns? How has painting in a small studio affected the scope of his work? And now his thinking, reading, writing, and painting will be shaped by new stimuli and new hobbies, like long walks, early nights and early mornings, bird watching, building and shaping his studio, and the quiet.

What are we to make of this move of the artist from the city to the country, from the urban center to the rural periphery, from community to isolation?

The city offers intense concentration. Artists can see great art in art museums, the newest art in galleries, and attend lectures and other social events that bring them into contact with artists, collectors, dealers, and critics. The art news cycle runs 24/7, and the institutions that are necessary for professional artistic practice are found in the city and are responsive to the latest developments.

Yet the blessing of intense concentration is also a curse. It can limit the scope of the artist's experience to seasonal fashions, force him to be responsive to what's perpetually new, often endowing the "next big thing" with a value it might not deserve. And the institutional, social aspects of artistic practice—going to events, meeting the right people—can gradually become the content of an artist's work, as he or she becomes an art world "insider" rather than an artist. In fact, cities can breed timidity among critics, curators, dealers, and artists who are fearful to go against fashion trends, upset convention, and risk marginalization from their peers, producing gestures toward risk but never quite actual risk taking.

For just as artists have by necessity worked in cities, in close proximity to patrons and an educated audience, many have lived at enmity with the city, and, at one time or another, have felt compelled to leave this battlefield of ambition and fear for the country. They have forsaken concentration for space—space to think, to work, to reconnect with nature, to detox from an addiction to art world gossip, to take off the blinders and drink more deeply from the waters of the living history of art, music, and literature that have endured over time.

Time away from the city allows the artist to make different artistic decisions, decisions not defined by workweek or season but the year or decade. For Fujimura, it allows him to transform a bucolic red barn into a spacious working studio, develop a bird-watching hobby, cultivate a garden, and take long walks with his wife and enjoy his grandchild.

The escape from the city is not an idealization of the country, as if it gets the artist closer to nature, or closer to God. In fact, it can do the opposite. It forces the artist to experience her exile anew, her distance from God, the world, and even herself. Art often contradicts our comfort with the world, reminding us that we are restless wanderers, and that the world is not as it should be. The city offers a place for wanderers to congregate together, and, at times, "exile" can become comfortable. The country forces the artist to once again confront his exile, and do so alone.

Art is about discontinuity and contradiction, which is how grace is experienced in the world: an alien intrusion into a world too used to telling us that we are defined by what we do, not by what we have received (1 Cor 4:7). And so we are compelled to prove ourselves, to make something that justifies our existence to God, the world, and ourselves. But art is not just doing and making; it is first receiving and hearing. It is the devotion of one's life to something so futile, inefficient, and in many ways useless, that it counterintuitively becomes a means of grace, a means of experiencing our humanity and individuality as a gift.

Cities, with their concentration of doers and achievers, with their narratives of do-it-yourself success stories full of those obsessed with going from good to great, can pose challenges to cultivating a passivity and receptivity that is absolutely necessary for artistic practice.

Nevertheless, the city is indispensable for artistic practice. An artist cannot develop without the concentration, the creative density that cities offer. And yet to make works of art that are not solely defined by contemporary fashions, locked into and responsive to parochial concerns, and with the stench of ambition, artists need to develop ways, at times, to escape it. Not every artist needs a Walden Pond or Fuji Farm. But every artist needs to step away from the urban pressure to do, to build, to transform, to engage.

The country can also offer a means by which the artist restores her work to the larger, more diverse fabric of work. The intense concentration in the city tends to narrow the artist's vocational vision—everyone she knows is an artist, critic, curator, and drawing a paycheck from the art world somehow, even if it is sitting at the reception desk at an art museum or working on an exhibition installation team. In the country, the artist befriends the mechanic, gets to know the dairy farmer or beekeeper down the road, and begins to think about making her paintings in the context of producing honey, milk, and getting the car to run. Munch often placed his precious paintings outside in the Norwegian cold in order to toughen them up, see how they would fare out in the real world of freezing rain and bird poop in order to see how they might stand up to nature. He thought it would "do them good to fend for themselves." The country seems to offer that experience for the artist herself. Can I still be an artist without the trappings, the comforts, the professional and emotional crutches, the insulation from challenges to my importance and relevance?

The artist who retreats to the country from the city is not surrendering in the heat of the battle. No, she is merely re-engaging it with a new arsenal.

REIMAGINING PATRONAGE

Patience is a rare commodity in the art world, which is driven by collectors, dealers, and curators who need immediate returns on their aesthetic investments. The contemporary art world seems less and less willing to acknowledge that history shows that the career of the artist is measured not by the May and November auction results but in *decades*. The establishment of aesthetic value takes time and often involves acts of historical retrieval.

The development of an artistic vision is achieved over a long arc. The Abstract Expressionist master Willem de Kooning painted *for twenty years* in New York before he had his first exhibition at the Charles Egan gallery in 1948. The obsession with the new and young has produced an environment in which an artist in her mid-forties, having worked in the art world for over twenty years, is too old to attract the attention of these taste-making collectors and their train of curators. This poses significant obstacles to the cultivation of an artistic vision, which demands space and time.

What can contradict the impatience and insecurity of the art world in which artists function as chips in a high-stakes cultural card game? Some artists, like Damien Hirst and Jeff Koons, have tried to join the game. Yet this strategy, as successful as I think it is in some respects, also works against their long-term development, since they are forced to treat their own work as chips, thereby granting the common assumption that their work is merely instrumental, the means by which they get to play with collectors, dealers, and curators. Moreover, it ultimately affirms rather than contradicts the impatience and insecurity in the art world.

Patronage is another strategy. Patronage creates space and gives artists time by defying the impatience of the art world by delaying or deferring a return on investment. A patron offers regular financial support for an artist that is based on the patron's belief that the artist is worth support, regardless of whether or not her work is in fashion. Patronage recognizes that artistic development is a long-term project. It forges the creative space that enables an artist to develop artistically without the fear that such development will destroy her career by scaring off collectors. It provides the financial stability to enable her to make work for an audience that is not limited to speculators. Patronage can thus provide the freedom that allows an artist *not* to have to make work for an exhibition at her gallery for the sole purpose of generating sales. *Patronage allows her the freedom to say "no."* It allows her the space and time to produce a writing project, do research, or read poetry—and produce artifacts that can't be sold by a dealer and resold at auction. In short, it enables the artist *not* to have to sell work to collectors to pay the bills or justify herself artistically through those transactions. Patronage allows the artist to grow and develop in ways that the market and the gallery structure cannot measure and cannot recognize.

Patronage is a means of grace. The patron offers resources to an artist whose work may not, according to the gallery-auction house network, merit it. By providing resources that open up creative space, the patron believes that the artist's work will, over time, attract the attention it deserves. In this way, patronage is an act of belief and an imputation of freedom for an artist who need not make work with the exclusive goal of finding a buyer. The patron believes that the artist's true audience for her work remains in the future.

The need for patronage in the art world is not a new idea. Frustrated by the art world, many cultural commentators—including many who hold Christian convictions—point to the role of the Renaissance and Counter-Reformation church as the model for a kind of artistic support that circumvents the precarious nature of the gallery-auction house network.

As instructive as those moments are, I would like to suggest that nineteenth- and twentieth-century modernism offers a more relevant model for contemporary patronage, one that works with and against markets of taste that are broader and more complicated than that of fifteenth-century Florence or sixteenth- and seventeenth-century Rome. Consequently, the relationship between patron and artist is less fraught with master-servant complexities, thus operating as a collaboration or partnership in the pursuit of shared goals across a complex institutional network. And these shared goals often consisted of undermining or circumventing existing social, cultural, and political structures. In the history of modernism, patronage is a form of cultural criticism, of pushing against dominant systems of value and distribution. We need to revive this idea of patronage as cultural criticism, as an embodiment of discontent with artistic business as usual, and a renewed and daring faith in the power of art.

And finally, patronage in the history of modernism ultimately consisted of helping to create the audience that the artist deserved, generating reception for an artist's work that embodied a new social vision. *Patronage works to achieve an audience over time.* This way of thinking about patronage is helpful in two ways.

First, it does not limit the role of the patron to a check-writer, one who simply offers financial means for this or that artist to pay for this or that project (flipping the Renaissance/Baroque master-slave roles). Too much discussion about patronage centers exclusively on finding the money to pay for the artist's little projects. The patron provides creative space for the artist to work without some of the financial pressures that are the fuel that runs the art world engine, but this space also allows for honest conversations between patron and artist and the development of a community of honest feedback and mutual conversation, liberated from the restrictions and anxieties of the gallery-auction house network, which artists rarely receive.

Second, it reveals that patronage, if it is primarily concerned to create an audience for an artist's work, also can and must include the curator, who stages exhibitions, and the critic who, through her words, contextualizes them. Often in the history of modern art the patron played the role of curator and critic as well. The audience who receives the artist's work must be achieved—created—through the efforts of patrons who believe deeply in the artist's vision, who are committed to marshaling all the resources necessary in order to put the work of that artist in front of that audience, an audience only to be realized fully in the future. And that requires curators, critics, and even gallery owners to serve as patrons, sacrificing short-term gain for long-term vision and commitment.

When I see Gustave Courbet's painting *The Source of the Loue* (1864) at the Metropolitan Museum of Art in New York, it exists for me at that moment because of the efforts of Courbet's collaborator and patron, Alfred Bruyas, whose significant financial, ideological, and creative support provided the space necessary for Courbet to paint against the Academy. However, it is also there before me because of the tireless efforts of other patrons, such as Proudhon and Jules Castagnary, Jules Champfleury, Charles Baudelaire, and other writers and thinkers who offered their talents for a time in order to create the Courbet whose painting confronts me.

Perhaps the time is right to reimagine patronage by rediscovering its important role in the history of modern art, as an embodiment of faith, that is, "the reality of what is hoped for, the proof of what is not seen" (Heb 11:1).

4

THE ARTIST

The goal of the artist is to deepen the mystery.

—Francis Bacon

A drawing is not foolishness, Papa.

—Asher Lev, in Chaim Potok, *My Name Is Asher Lev*

THE ARTIST, THE WORK OF ART, AND THE FREEDOM OF THE UNFREE WILL

What is the relationship of the work of art to the artist? Is it simply the sum of the artist's intentions—an aesthetic extension of the artist's emotions, thoughts, world view? Can the artist's life (his beliefs or actions) invalidate or destroy the integrity of the work he makes? Or does the work of art bear no relation to the artist's biography whatsoever? These are questions that have long occupied the attention of critics and scholars. An article published last summer in *The New York Times* offered another, if heartbreaking, perspective on this perplexing question of artistic intention.

In "Good Art, Bad People," Charles McGrath focuses his attention on writers who have produced great art but have done so at the expense of their loved ones.[1] He reflects on this disjunction and asks, how can we appreciate the great work of greatly flawed men and women? Hemingway is his primary focus but it could have been many others, like David Foster Wallace. Do their lives, that is, their immoral or criminal behavior, bigoted beliefs, and horrible treatment of friends and family, disqualify the greatness of their work? Are we obligated to experience a work of art through the biography of the artist and interpret it as an artifact of their broken lives (and ideas)? Most Christian reflection on the arts is shaped by the concept of "world view," that is, the belief that the Christian faith is, as Abraham Kuyper called Calvinism, "a comprehensive life system," a system that is essentially cognitive and rational that is applied to discrete examples—like works of art.[2] World view thinking therefore presumes that human action—like works of art—is determined by thought and so the meaning of those actions and artifacts can be traced back to thought. But when we Christians praise Hemingway for the austere beauty of his prose and the profound theological depth of his stories, how then do we respond to what one of his children, quoted in McBride's article, had to say about his work as a writer?

> In November 1952, just after his 21st birthday, Gregory, the youngest (and arguably most talented) of Hemingway's three children, wrote to his father: "When it's all added up, papa, it will be: he wrote a few good stories, had a novel and fresh approach to reality and he destroyed five persons—Hadley, Pauline, Marty [Martha Gelhorn, Hemingway's third wife], Patrick and possibly myself. Which do you think is the most important, your self-centered shit, the stories or the people?"

McBride then observes,

> There is no possibly about it: Gregory, the most damaged of all the Hemingway offspring, died, an alcoholic transvestite, in the Miami-Dade Women's Detention Center.

This chilling example takes the question of the relationship of the artist's life to the work of art to its ultimate end: does the production of a great work of art demand human sacrifice? And, perhaps even more horrifying, a sacrifice taken from the artist's own family and circle of friends?

Allowing this question to sit in the back of our minds, let's explore in more depth the relationship of an artist's intentions to the works of art she produces. A common assumption, of which Christian world view thinking is but one expression, presumes that a work of art is a direct extension, or

1. McGrath, "Good Art, Bad People."

2. Kuyper, *Lectures on Calvinism*, 9–40.

causal result, of the artist's thoughts, emotions, and/or beliefs. In fact, it is presumed to be so causally determined—the epistemological line so taught between the artist and work of art—that we are able to discern the artist's world view (her own "comprehensive life system") from her poem, novel, or painting. As the artist's beliefs go, so goes the work of art.

We want artists to tell us, once for all, "what the painting means," yet this is contrary to how artists understand their work. Art fights against this causality. Abstract Expressionist painter Willem de Kooning once said that he painted himself out of a picture and T. S. Eliot observed that the meaning of a poem occurred somewhere between the poem and the reader. The artist brings all she has to the production of a particular work—emotions, thoughts, ideas, both conscious and unconscious—but the work then faces the world and moves toward the viewer, reader, listener. W. H. Auden said somewhere that he thought that the artist's biography wasn't important in understanding a work of art because the artist pours "everything" he has and is into the work, and "biography" presupposes that only certain parts of an artist's life impact it. For Auden, to talk about the artist's biography or even his "intentions" is to demean or trivialize his presence in the work, a presence that defies even the artist's attempt to isolate it.

When we read a poem or look at a painting, it is not the artist but the work of art that is working on us, and what it offers to us is therefore much broader and deeper than the artist's intentions and beliefs, many of which she is only barely aware, if at all.

Andres Serrano's controversial and notorious photograph *Piss Christ* (1987) offers an interesting example. It came to public attention as Republicans led an agenda to defund the National Endowment for the Arts and became an icon for artists receiving federal funding in order to "undermine" the nation's "values." (Although the cultural politics involved in Serrano's *Piss Christ* are too vast to summarize here, suffice it to say that the issue was not about the experience of a work of art and the complex range of feelings it produced in viewers.)[3]

The photograph is part of a series of works Serrano produced by submerging mass-manufactured kitsch artifacts, both religious (Mary, Jesus, crucifixes) and classical (male and female Greco-Roman torsos), in large Plexiglas containers filled with urine and blood. *Piss Christ* is distinctive because the sharpness of the title, which feels almost blasphemous, is contradicted by the beauty and elegance of the photograph itself, even though it was produced by bodily waste. As it is an icon of the culture wars, both the Left and the Right presume *Piss Christ* to be a "statement" by Serrano

---

3. See my "*Piss Christ* Revisited" in this volume.

on his views of Christianity. But the case is not that simple. Serrano's own statements about the piece shifted and changed over time and in response to the shrill and uncivil discourse around it, from nuanced and ambivalent to polemical and categorical. But *Piss Christ* itself has generated diverse responses, negative and positive, from Christians and non-Christians, which testifies to the fact that the work speaks in ways that transcend and surpass what Serrano has said about it.

This gap, however slight and tenuous, between the work of art and artist (his life, thoughts, and intentions) is crucial to maintain, not only for aesthetic but for theological reasons. It is based on the artist's unfree will. We are trained to believe that art is about the expression of freedom. Although few would put it quite this way, artists intuitively recognize that they possess a radically unfree will. One of its many consequences is that it makes even one's own heart a mystery. If my will is not free, my intentions, desires, and thoughts cannot be transparent to me, much less to anyone else. And artists, through their own studio practices, recognize this. Artists make paintings, poems, stories, and music not to express what they already know and feel (celebration of a free will) but to try to discover something about themselves they do not know. The work of art thus encompasses more of the artist than he or she is even consciously aware. Indeed their work is an attempt to search those unfathomable and mysterious depths—both conscious and unconscious—of their own hearts and their own understanding. Scripture offers plenty of evidence that supports the Prophet Jeremiah's lament, "The heart is deceitful above all things, and desperately sick; who can understand it?" (Jer 17:9).

One of the problems of Christian world view thinking is that it presupposes that human beings, especially artists, are consciously aware and in rational possession of their intentions, desires, thoughts, and goals—in short, it presupposes that the human heart is transparent to its owner. Artists, more than anyone else, are confronted with the convoluted mystery and frustrating opacity (and darkness) of one's own heart, the impossibility of knowing one's own intentions and living an entirely consistent "world view." (No human being is a "nihilist," "humanist," "atheist," or even "Christian" all the time—Paul and Luther emphasize the battle between the old Adam and the new Adam.) Artists know they work with a radically unfree will when they finish a painting, stand back to look at it, and realize it is doing something they not only did not expect but could not control, yet also revealing something profound about their experience. Artists follow St. Paul, who made much of the war inside himself, that maddening disjunction between what he wanted and what actually occured, the confrontation of the old and the new Adam (Rom 7:21–25), which made him incapable even to judge his own intentions (1 Cor 4:3–4).

That we do not and cannot know our hearts is a source of liberation for those who know that their hearts are known fully only in Christ (1 Cor 13: 12). And it is what gives great works of art their capacity to transcend the limits of their makers and their deceitful hearts—and perhaps even plumb the depths of those hearts in ways that elude their understanding, opening up a space that allows the viewer, reader, or listener to discover unknown regions of their own hearts. Contrary to everything we've been taught, the very existence of art is a witness to our unfree wills and a promise that they will one day be free.

While we lament the tragic disjunction between the darkness of Hemingway's life and the light of his work, we can give thanks nevertheless for that light, which shows us, if only momentarily, beauty in the face of ugliness, clarity in the face of chaos, and freedom in the face of slavery. Yet while we celebrate that light, we would do well to remember the cost of its existence in the world when we pull a book by Hemingway off the shelf.

But it is not just Hemingway's problem. Do we really know and are fully aware of the damage our work does to our families—even the work we claim is "good," the work we believe we're doing for the kingdom? While art reminds us that our wills are unfree, our hearts a mystery to us, and we are largely ignorant of the consequences of our actions on our friends and family, we can rest in the promise that in Christ *all things* will be reconciled, even the heartbreaking contradiction between Hemingway's stories and the pain he caused his children, between my work and the pain I cause the ones I love (Col 1: 20).

THE OTHER WARHOL[4]

There are times when an artist is crushed by popularity, notoriety, or infamy, and art museum exhibitions often serve to create space for the artist's legacy to breathe and expand beyond the restrictive confines of public perception. And for American artists, it is often European art museums that provide that opportunity. In 2001 German curator Heiner Bastian organized *Andy Warhol Retrospective* for the Neue Nationalgalerie in Berlin. Featuring over 250 works, after opening in Berlin and traveling to the Tate Modern in London, the exhibition traveled to the Museum of Contemporary Art in Los Angeles (MoCA), offering the most comprehensive exhibition of Warhol's

---

4. A version of this review was previously published in *Books and Culture* (November-December 2002).

work in the United States in over thirty years. The exhibition and the catalogue that accompanied it offer a deeper understanding of one of the most important artists of the twentieth century.

But even to say that Warhol's art requires a deeper understanding and that he has importance for us is to pick a fight. More than any other contemporary artist, Warhol is an artist we love to hate—perhaps the most notorious yet least understood artist of his time. He seems to represent either everything good or everything bad about art and culture in the United States since the 1960s.

The response from Christians committed to art has tended to fall along party lines. For liberal Catholics and for Protestants influenced by Paul Tillich, for whom high art was by definition transcendent, Warhol is cryptospiritualist. They call attention to his Byzantine Catholic upbringing and his faithful attendance at mass. For conservative Christians the response is nearly a mirror opposite. Warhol the homosexual, huckster, and publicity hound, whose studio, which he called the Factory, came to embody the libertine creed of the sixties, delivered the coup de grace that finally killed art's remaining transcendent value.

There's more than just a grain of truth to these rival versions of Warhol: the celebrity, the decadent, the postmodern saint. But the Warhol on display in the exhibition and revealed in the scholarship included in the catalogue is someone else. The power of this other Warhol was undeniable, even in Los Angeles, where the context predisposed visitors to experience him through the lens of celebrity and notoriety.

Who is this other Warhol?

Bastian's exhibition is an attempt to decontextualize Warhol, to disengage him from his reputation and his standing as a paradigmatic American. He is eager to present Warhol's oeuvre as worthy of aesthetic experience and critical analysis on its own terms, not as an illustration of the culture wars, which is largely the American response to the artist. For Bastian and his colleagues, the mystery and profundity of Warhol's work has been stripped. His work has been too easily "explained" by his homosexuality, his Catholicism, his interest in commercial art, his love of American popular culture, his connections to the music, fashion, and entertainment industry, and so on.

What happens if we set all that aside and attend to the work itself, to give it space to breathe and speak to us? What emerges, it seems to me, is an artist whose work is concerned primarily with the presence of death.

After graduating from the Carnegie Institute of Technology, Warhol went to New York in 1949 in search of work as a commercial artist. Not only did he find work; he became one of the most sought-after and influential commercial artists of the fifties. But as the decade waned, Warhol increasingly turned to large-scale paintings of popular imagery, abandoning the world of *haute couture* for the "crudely anonymous, out-of-date tasteless trash" found in low-end newspapers and magazines. Warhol's move from commercial art to studio art, from advertising to fine art, allowed him the opportunity to address in his creative work what was forbidden him by the fashion industry, with its obsession with youth, virility, and their accouterments: death.

Whether experienced as a coming final judgment or as a constant reminder of the existence of what Tillich called ultimate concerns, death contradicts the materialism and technology of consumerism that defines fashion and advertising. The art exhibition in SoHo rather than the boutique display case on Madison Avenue became the means by which Warhol could address death in his studio work. And in fact his entire body of work seems to be an elaboration of the eighteenth-century *vanitas* still life tradition, in which the material pleasures of life (food, drink, and other expressions of wealth) are simultaneously celebrated in their beauty and goodness and yet revealed to be ultimately temporary, passing away. "Vanity of vanities," the Preacher in Ecclesiastes writes, "all is vanity."

Perhaps the clearest example of this reorientation can be found in his notorious *Campbell's Soup Cans*, exhibited at the Ferus Gallery in Los Angeles in 1962. Painting by hand from a retailer's catalogue, Warhol attempted to reproduce individually the labels for each of the company's thirty-two flavors, creating what Kirk Varnedoe calls an "uneven quirkiness."[5]

At the time, Campbell's soup was an extraordinary model of stability. Its label design and price had not changed for over fifty years. In the eyes of many interpreters of Warhol's work, it stood for the stifling banality of mainstream America. But Warhol was not making fun of Campbell's soup, or the culture that produced it (his mother fed him it every day at lunch when he was growing up in a working-class neighborhood). Ultimately, Varnedoe, the former director of painting and sculpture at the Museum of Modern Art, New York (MoMA), where these paintings now are located, concludes:

> No summation or paraphrase anyone will ever write of it, nor any theoretical web to be spun around it, is ever even remotely likely to be anything like the panoply of things it effortlessly is all at once: hot, cold, heartless, funny, lively, boring, sad, outrageous, economical, memorable, vicious, stupid, sophisticated, crass and more.[6]

5. Varnedoe, "Campbell's Soup Cans, 1962," in Bastian, ed., *Andy Warhol*, 43.
6. Ibid, 45.

While *Campbell's Soup Cans* (which unfortunately did not travel to Los Angeles for the exhibition) provides a link from his early career as a commercial artist to his work as a fine artist, the MoCA exhibition shows the important role that Warhol's so-called disaster paintings and prints played in his oeuvre after the Ferus Gallery exhibition of soup cans in 1962. In fact, these "disaster" pieces, beginning in 1963 with his monumental *129 Die in Jet* and including recurring images of suicides, electric chairs, guns, knives, car crashes, and skulls, give Warhol's entire body of work a tragic vision of which I was not completely aware before this exhibition but now see it as obviously saturating his entire body of work. Even his iconic images of Jackie Kennedy and Marilyn Monroe, often read as clichés of beauty and fashion, are marked by death: Jackie was mourning her husband's death when Warhol depicted her serene beauty, and he made the Marilyn prints after she had committed suicide. There is a profound tension between the beautiful surfaces of Warhol's (often gigantic) works and the underlying tragedy of death, the loss that always lingers over the shoulder of beauty or which brings it forth.

Peter-Klaus Schuster's essay in the catalogue makes this explicit. In "Warhol and Goya," he compares the Spaniard's famous "Disasters of War" etchings to Warhol's "disasters of peace." Schuster argues that "Death holds court at the very heart of the consumer paradise; consumerism is the modern Vanitas, with the sanction of the market economy."[7] That death "holds court" is because consumerism is itself a response to it, a means to contradict, fight, or forget it. If readers find incompatible Schuster's attempt to interpret Warhol's work within the context of the *vanitas* tradition—within a pictorial tradition in which what is experienced in culture is merely a transitory pleasure—consider that Goya advertised his "Disasters of War" etchings in a local newspaper and sold them at a perfume and liquor store in Madrid.

Warhol's most powerful and haunting disaster images are those of the anonymous young men and women, captured by photojournalists, who died in car accidents or suicides. Warhol spent countless hours in police station archives sifting through these images, and said that he thought it important to memorialize these nameless people, whom he found by combing through newspapers and photo archives. These images are infused with a somber humanity strikingly at odds with the celebrity culture that adores Warhol (and which, it must be said, he helped to create). Warhol's disasters, Schuster says, are best understood "not as a critique of a callous, unjust society but as a critique of the media message, and of the attendant desensitization and

---

7. Schuster, "Warhol and Goya," in Bastian, ed., *Andy Warhol*, 55.

dehumanization of public consciousness."[8] And, I would suggest, a reassertion of the integrity of the individual, even and perhaps especially in death. These large-scale, haunting works become a means by which the clinical documentation of photojournalism for eyes that desire only "reality" and "the facts" is transformed into evocative aesthetic experiences formed by the history of art that do not deny the presence of death or gawk at it voyeuristically, but acknowledge its tragic presence not only in the lives of the victims but in our own.

We presume that Warhol's claim that "in the future everyone will be famous for fifteen minutes" was his mission statement. Not so. Warhol was bemoaning the loss of individuality under the impact of mass media. Elsewhere, he observed, "Some day everybody will think just what they want to think, and then everybody will probably be thinking alike; that seems to be what is happening."[9] Surprisingly, death was the means by which Warhol reaffirmed our individuality. Martin Luther described the human experience, no matter religious creed, when he said, "The summons of death comes to us all, and no one can die for another. Every one must fight his own battle with death by himself, alone."[10] Yet the cultural patterns and social conventions of the modern world enable us to deny this most lonely of endeavors. This is why theologian Oswald Bayer observes, "we must be told who we are"—and who we are are creatures who will die, and will do so alone.[11] The *vanitas* artistic tradition is one of the means by which a more authentic individuality—one based on receiving life and its limits as a gift—can be built emotionally, through paint.

Varnedoe's conclusion about Warhol's *Campbell's Soup Cans* is applicable to the artist's entire body of work: "art does not need to be deep to be profound."[12] Warhol's work also shows how art, which explores the creeping loss of individuality in a culture that claims to celebrate it and the lurking presence of death even in a culture which actively denies it, does not have to have traditional religious content to be profoundly theological. As George Steiner has written, to experience art is a risk, for we offer art—an artifact of another's intentionality, their humanity—the run of our house, challenging us in ways we cannot even conceive by gaining access to the "freedom of our inner city."[13] In a trendy contemporary art space in the most self-consciously

8. Ibid.

9. Quoted in Bastian, ed., *Andy Warhol*, 58.

10. Quoted in Bayer, "The Modern Narcissus," 306–7.

11. Bayer, *Freedom in Response*, 54.

12. Varnedoe, "Campbell's Soup Cans, 1962," in Bastian, ed., *Andy Warhol*, 45.

13. Steiner, *Real Presences*, 185.

hip and oppressively fashion-paranoid city in the world, the works on the walls, in their overwhelming totality, had their way with my "inner city." I look forward to learning what this other Warhol will do to me as an art historian, curator, and Christian.

THE DARK LIGHT OF THOMAS KINKADE

In *The Idiot* (1869), Dostoyevsky's Prince Mishkin notices a reproduction of Holbein's *Dead Christ* on the wall in Rogozhin's house, and observes that it has the power to make one lose their Christian faith. The painting is unusual because Holbein painted it in the form of a predella, which forms the base of an altarpiece, featuring Christ's crucifixion and resurrection. But there is no altarpiece to put Holbein's dead Christ in context. Mishkin's fear is that without the context of the resurrection provided by the altarpiece, the dead Christ deprives the Christian of hope. Because Holbein's painting offers no resurrection, it cannot proclaim anything but a death with unrelenting power, enough to vanquish even the Son of God. Dostoyevsky was fascinated with the painting the first time he saw it in Basel, and apparently his wife had to pull him away from it after hours of close inspection. No doubt Dostoyevsky was fascinated by the implications of the image of God's body beginning to decay. Holbein gives us perhaps the most terrifying painting of death in the Western tradition, a death that kills even God himself, a death with no resurrection to distract us from its finality.

It is also a reminder. The *Dead Christ* is at the heart of all painting, even at the heart of all the work of our hands (Ps 90:1). For we live east of Eden. We have been driven from the garden and it remains to this day guarded by a cherubim with a flaming sword to prevent our return (Gen 3: 24), which we feel, regardless of religious belief, in the inescapable presence of death, loneliness, and futility. All the work that we do comes from this wound. And art in the modern tradition foregrounds this wound.

Yet Thomas Kinkade, who died on Good Friday in 2012, made pictures that might be more terrifying than Holbein's, giving us a world deprived not only of Easter Sunday, but Holy Saturday, Good Friday, and thus Christ himself. Kinkade is known to have claimed, "I like to portray a world without the Fall." And so Kinkade's work is a refusal to work east of Eden.

My professional colleagues in the art world have long dismissed Kinkade's work as harmlessly trite, uninteresting, nostalgic, and sentimental illustrations that provide consumers with an "art-like" experience without the rigors and demand of attending rigorously to learning the tradition of serious art. And I agree. Looking at serious painting, reading serious poetry, or listening to serious music requires work and practice to master its tradition, a tradition that claims that a work of art speaks and the viewer has a responsibility to listen, and perhaps, to be changed.

But Kinkade refuses to participate in this tradition. And so his images prey on his audience's preconceptions, expectations, and presumptions, restricting rather than broadening or deepening their experience. These are problems that are not merely Kinkade's. They infect a large swath of the contemporary art world as well. But from a theological perspective, his work is not merely problematic, it is dangerous. Kinkade has long railed against the nihilism of modern art and the contemporary art world. But because it claims to deny where we live, that is, in the midst of death and brokenness, east of Eden, Kinkade's work is more nihilistic than anything Picasso and Pollock could paint, or Nietzsche and Sartre could write. Chaim Potok speaks for the modern tradition of art when Jacob Kahn warns his student Asher Lev:

> I see the world as hard-edged, filled with lines and angles. And I see it as wild and raging and hideous, and only occasionally beautiful. The world fills me with disgust more often than it fills me with joy. Are you listening to me Asher Lev? The world is a terrible place. I do not sculpt and paint to make the world sacred. I sculpt and paint to give permanence to my feelings about how terrible this world truly is.[14]

As dark and morbid as this description is, it describes our reality east of Eden. And yet, artists sharing Jacob Kahn's view of art and the world believed that art offered—or could offer—some kind of redemption, some kind of salvation. And so artistic practice itself was considered to be a kind of confession of faith.

Not so for Kinkade. Because it denies the reality of death, evil, and sin, his work is unable to offer hope. Because it is an outgrowth of his (imagined) view of a world "before the Fall," a world in which he ignores the angels that guard the gates of Eden and returns, Kinkade depicts a world that on the surface appears to be ideal. But the Edenic world Kinkade represents is pretty much the fallen world without the dirtiness of the city and the inconvenience of other people. It feels like a weekend getaway in the country. All we need to do to return to Eden is get our lives in order with some time away. Kinkade's much-ballyhooed "light" merely adds atmosphere and glow, a pleasant touch to an already charming scene. And because it makes us so comfortable and allows us to imagine Eden to be not too much unlike our reality, only without some inconveniences, it is a very dark light indeed.

14. Potok, *My Name is Asher Lev*, 209.

Kinkade's work, then, is like a meticulously painted smile on the Joker's disfigured face. It refuses to deal with the fallenness, brokenness, and sinfulness of the world and the wound of our expulsion from Eden, the wound of sin, idolatry, unbelief. His images enable his clientele to escape into an imaginary world where things can be pretty good, as long as we have our faith, our family values, and a visual imagery that reaffirms all this at the office and at home. Kinkade's work, for all its apparent harmlessness, has overpowered the cherubim that stand guard over the garden.

One of the chief virtues of the best art in the Western tradition—especially modern art—is that it cuts through our self-deception to show us who were are and where we stand. It tells us who we are by telling us, as the marble statue of Apollo in Rilke's famous poem, "you must change your life!" Art can remind us that we don't just need a boost, a change of scenery, or a weekend getaway. We need to be killed so that we can be raised again. Art can and should at times kill us, destroying our pretensions to virtue, goodness, and our desire to enlist art in our own self-improvement schemes that violate the cherubim standing guard. The literary critic George Steiner wrote:

> Serious painting, music, literature or sculpture make palpable
> to us, as do no other means of communication, the unassuaged,
> unhoused instability and estrangement of our condition.[15]

This "estrangement," however, often brings with it a hope for reconciliation, an intuition, perhaps only as an aesthetic experience, that there is a "deeper magic" than death, that somehow it too may be swallowed up. And so perhaps Holbein's *Dead Christ*, a predella without a resurrection, is necessary, forcing us to dwell in Holy Saturday, to contemplate death, not just as an abstraction, but also as the continual oppressive reality that it is. And that life—hope, love, grace—can only come *through* it.

But Kinkade's work refuses to take us to the end of ourselves, refuses the confrontations and disruption that could open us up to grace. His images give us a world that's really okay, a world in which all we need is home and hearth, a weekend retreat, a cozy night with the family to put us right with God. It is a world devoid of pain and suffering; devoid of any fear of insanity or suicide; devoid of making an image that actually connects with the pain and suffering of his clients and offers hope. It is a world in which we follow St. Peter and rebuke Jesus for his claim that he must die (Mark 8: 31–33).

15. Steiner, *Real Presences,* 139.

As a result, it is also a world without grace, and without the Word that offers it, *through death*. Kinkade's multimillion-dollar empire was built on our fallen human refusal to confront our innate hopelessness and our need to do what the Ninevites did in the book of Jonah: rip our clothes, put on sackcloth and ashes, and beg for God's grace. "Who knows? God may turn and relent and turn from his fierce anger, so that we may not perish" (Jonah 3: 9).

Although his visual imagery refused to acknowledge violence and desperation, Kinkade's personal life was full of it— drug and alcohol addiction, destroyed personal and professional relationships, and legal battles. Making imagery from Eden, he lived east of it. I can only imagine the excruciating pressure he felt to live up to these deceptively dangerous images, images which deprived him of the grace he so desperately needed by refusing him the freedom to paint what he felt and experienced.

Although it was a weak heart and too much alcohol that caused his sudden death at fifty-four on Good Friday in 2012, the unrelenting pressure that the production and distribution of these reality-denying images exerted on a man who spent thirty years trying to live up to their impossible and inhuman standard must have contributed to it. His emotional life found no creative release in and through his studio work. As he, like each of us, experienced the ebb and flow of life—the challenges, tragedies, and the struggle with personal demons—he was forced (condemned) to produce the same innocuously nostalgic pictures again and again, fighting on one hand to preserve a brand as the Painter of Light, while he fought to the death his own demons on the other. If only Kinkade could have used his considerable artistic gifts to produce work from his fear, anger, desperation, and his struggle with faith in Christ, he just might have become a painter of Light.

VELÁZQUEZ, MODERN ART, AND THE DETACHMENT OF GRACEFUL PAINTING

Some time ago an artist friend, knowing that I had been thinking about José Ortega y Gasset's theory of modern art in *The Dehumanization of Art* (1925), gave me an obscure little book on six paintings in the Prado by Spanish Baroque master Diego Velázquez (1599–1660), which included an introductory essay by Ortega y Gasset. He also passed on to me a discovery he had made about Velázquez on a recent trip to the Prado in Madrid, where many of the great painter's paintings are housed, along with the collection of paintings that Velázquez himself had amassed for his friend and employer King Phillip IV. While studying Velázquez's pictures my friend found evidence that the artist had actually used corners of his canvases to clean his brush—an act that appears at once supremely confident and yet somehow detached, as if painting did not matter to him, or at least matter in the same way that it did to others. My artist friend, himself a painter, thought that Ortega y Gasset's essay suggested a way to think about this rather unusual discovery and what it might mean.

Velázquez's Personality

Velázquez, who is one of the great portrait painters in the Western tradition, clearly interests Ortega y Gasset. Like a number of other artists, critics, and philosophers, Ortega y Gasset sees in Velázquez's work a foretaste of a modernism to come.[16] But he locates the origins of the influence in an unlikely source.

What Ortega y Gasset finds extraordinary and determinative in the shape of his career that will influence the art of the nineteenth and twentieth centuries are two unusual features about his personal life. The first is that he led a remarkably uneventful "humdrum" life, as Ortega y Gasset calls it. Hired by Phillip IV as court painter at twenty-three years of age, Velázquez lived his entire life in the confines of the palace. His personal life was also defined by fidelity and unusual contentment. Ortega y Gasset observes, "There was but one woman in his life—his wife; but one friend—the King; but one workroom—the palace."[17] An artist, Ortega y Gasset writes, often "requires the pressure exerted by a troubled life, just as a lemon must be squeezed before it yields its juice."[18] But Velázquez's life seems almost entirely devoid of such pressure.

The second feature is that "Velázquez was an artist whose distinction was not based upon painting, but, one might be tempted to say, upon painting little."[19] This is because, despite his extraordinary talent, Velázquez was not all that interested in painting. In fact, Ortega y Gasset argues that he "disclaimed his artistic vocation" because he "did not want, never wanted, to be a painter" and he considered the act of painting to be simply "the execution of sovereign orders."[20] This is all the more remarkable given Ve-

---

16. Foucault, *The Order of Things*; Fried, *Manet's Modernism or the Face of Painting in the 1860s*; Tinterow, ed., *Manet/Velázquez*.

17. Ortega y Gasset, "Introduction," in *Six Color Reproductions by Diego Velázquez in the Prado Museum*, 6.

18. Ibid., 12.

19. Ibid., 7.

20. Ibid., 10.

lázquez's genius as a painter, a genius that, according to Ortega y Gasset, was already fully formed before he was hired by the king. Velázquez seemed unconcerned to display this genius and unthreatened by the professional jealousies that emerged from rival painters who resented the fact that painting came so easily to him. He painted rapidly and with such grace that he rarely made studies for his paintings, choosing rather to compose directly on the canvas, and although he painted very quickly, he would leave paintings unfinished for long periods of time.

Although it came so easily to him, Velázquez rarely painted. His biographers have argued that this was because he was so busy carrying out the king's business at court and throughout Europe. But Ortega y Gasset denies the validity of this argument. And in fact, he suggests precisely the opposite: "never had a painter more time than Velázquez," whom he calls a "multi-millionaire of time." It was not just simply because he didn't have many paintings to make; it was also how he experienced time. This is how Ortega y Gasset puts it: "One, in spite of always being in a hurry, never has time enough. Another, in spite of all the haste, disregards it, filling it with placidity within which life becomes effortless."[21]

This "placidity," or "apathy," as Ortega y Gasset calls it, would seem to be disastrous to the capacity of the artist to make compelling work. He lived in isolation in the palace, surrounded by his own work and the Italian and Flemish masters he acquired for his boss and friend. He refused commissions and getting involved in promoting his work, getting embroiled in the usual controversies, to be burdened by insecurities that affect other artists. "Sated by his own talent," Ortega y Gasset argues, "Velazquez lived beyond the opinion of the untalented. Not only did he decline to defend himself against envy, but he also failed to do anything to spread and broaden his fame."[22] The result of all of this was that he was relatively unknown throughout his lifetime. Indeed, it was not until the middle of the nineteenth century with Manet's "rediscovery" of him that Velázquez became the unquestioned master he is considered today.

What Ortega y Gasset suggests about Velázquez is unprecedented in the history of art—Velázquez's colossal genius as a painter, combined with role as court painter and his lack of interest in painting as a vocation, meant that *he did not have to paint*, neither from financial nor psychological necessity. He never had to choose between his family and his art, sacrifice one for the other, or experience them as enemies, as in Potok's *My Name is Asher*

21. Ibid., 7.
22. Ibid., 8.

Lev and *The Gift of Asher Lev*, or, more tragically, Hemingway's son's accusation that his father "wrote a few good stories" but "destroyed five persons."[23]

In contrast to many if not most artists in the Western tradition whom we consider great, Velázquez did not locate his identity or justify his existence through his remarkable gifts as a painter, gifts that apparently required no sacrifices from him, and gifts he exercised as infrequently as possible. From the portrait of the artist that Ortega y Gasset paints, no artist seems to have cared less about his craft than Velázquez, much less avoided suffering the many emotional consequences that we believe drive creative work. His contemporaries were enraged by his ambivalence, the ease with which he painted, his refusal to engage them and solicit patrons and commissions, and how unimpressed he seemed to be by his own achievements.

Portraiture and Distance

What kind of effect did this peculiar personality and approach to life and his gift have on Velázquez's work itself? Ortega y Gasset writes, "After having rid his painting activities of everything smacking of professional coercion, he was able to face art from a distance."[24] Velázquez's "distance," or perhaps better, detachment, toward life expressed itself in a particular kind of aesthetic detachment in his paintings, both in subject matter and style.

Velázquez not only refused to solicit or accept commissions, but he also refused to paint the historical and religious subjects that featured heroes from classical and biblical literature and which traditionally established an artist's reputation. With few exceptions, he was content to paint portraits—a genre long considered to be of secondary importance. Yet, in his hands, it was transformed, setting the stage for its dominance in the modern tradition. Ortega y Gasset writes, "This revolution consisted in turning all painting into portraiture—that is, individualizing the object and rendering the scene as a single momentary event."[25] This "revolution" coincided with his belief that

> Velázquez felt at the very core of his being what nobody before him had felt and what clearly meant an anticipation of the future: a satiety with beauty and poetry, a hunger for prose. Prose is the form of maturity achieved by art after long experiences with the game of poetry.[26]

23. Quoted in McGrath, "Good Art, Bad People."
24. Ortega y Gasset, "Introduction," 13.
25. Ortega y Gasset, "Velázquez and His Fame," in *Velázquez*, 25.
26. Ortega y Gasset, "Introduction," 18.

The portraits that Velázquez painted were indeed prosaic. In addition to the portraits of the royal family, he painted *bodegones*, that is, scenes in taverns and kitchens that feature subjects from the lower classes, and portraits of the servants and other staff in the royal court with which he interacted on a daily basis, transforming even these banal subjects into portraits, for, according to Ortega y Gasset, every painting Velázquez painted was a portrait since a "painting is portraiture if it undertakes to define the individuality of the object."[27] What seemed to interest him, then, were the people he knew, observed, respected, and loved. His distance, his emotional detachment from art and its ambition, seems to have allowed him the freedom to paint these often-overlooked subjects, considered prosaic, banal, "ugly" with imperfections, and yet infuse them with profound humanity and dignity.

What Velázquez Painted

Art historians and theorists regard Velázquez's masterpiece *Las Meninas* (1656) to be one of the first modern paintings, a painting about painting, a painting about vision, a painting that undermines the viewer's identity as a stable, unified subject.[28] The composition is a portrait of the king and queen's daughter as the artist himself is in the process of painting it. There are two gratuitous elements in a painting that is about the royal family and the artist that paints them. The dog and the dwarf seize our attention—the dog is one of the most magnificent animals depicted in any painting, capturing the nobility, fidelity, and contentment of a creature clearly adored by the entourage, unfazed even by a bit of childish heckling. The dwarf is also represented with dignity, as she is the only one of the group who notices and addresses the viewer along with the artist. The presence of the dog and the dwarf transform the painting from a "poetic" royal portrait (the king and queen are even included as reflections in a background mirror) to a "prosaic" *bodegones* composition.

Velázquez painted many dwarfs, depicting them with considerable dignity. They are portraits, affirming the individuality of the subject, worthy of a name, a psychological investigation. And Velázquez treats them as bearing God's image, revealing them to be as intelligent, wise, and experienced as any person in the court.

And yet it is difficult to ignore that something else is happening. Because Velázquez has such a detached and prosaic view of life, it is possible to consider these portraits of dwarfs to be *representative* of a human condition,

27. Ibid., 14.
28. See Foucault, *The Order of Things*.

stripped of its pretense of beauty, honor, strength, power, and wealth. Rather than lifting up the dwarfs, Velázquez is bringing the wealthy, the powerful, and the beautiful down. Ortega y Gasset calls Velázquez, "a marvelous painter of ugliness."[29] For Ortega y Gasset, the "ugly" simply means the prosaic, the banal, the imperfect, before it has been "perfected," idealized, and elevated by the poetry of art. Moreover, "it would also mean preserving the fleeting values of a reality which bears death and disintegration within itself."[30]

The dwarf discloses the human condition more honestly and directly than do the kings, dukes, and ambassadors. And this is also evidenced in many of Velázquez's portraits of his friend and king, Phillip IV, who exhibits a vulnerability, discomfort, and naiveté that is in stark contrast to the determined confidence of one of Velázquez's most powerful portraits, the dwarf *Sebastian de Morra* (1643–44), who exhibits a virility and gravitas that belies his childish pose (he's seated on the ground with his legs outstretched).

How Velázquez Painted

Velázquez's profound, unprecedented detachment was manifest most clearly for Ortega y Gasset, however, in *how* he painted. Ortega y Gasset suggests that Velázquez's distinctively loose brushwork "ignored the corporal nature of his subjects" by eschewing the dramatic plays of light and shadow, called chiaroscuro, which affirmed the sculptural and tactile aspects of the subject.[31] Velázquez's was a painting of "pure visibility."[32]

If this begins to sound like how modernist formalist art critics of the twentieth century like Roger Fry, Cleve Grey, and Clement Greenberg wrote about abstraction, it is because Ortega y Gasset sees in Velázquez's aesthetic distance the seeds of modern art, what he would call its "dehumanization," that is, as a stylistic means by which the artist detaches the viewer from reality so that the painting, instead of being used as an instrument to help the viewer think about her concerns, her attachments, her burdens, becomes the very object of her thinking.[33]

29. Ortega y Gasset, "Velázquez and His Fame," 18.
30. Ibid., 13.
31. Ibid.
32. Ortega y Gasset, "Introduction," 15.
33. Ortega y Gasset, *The Dehumanization of Art,* 19.

Art for Art's Sake

By contrasting art to the realities of life, Ortega y Gasset is offering a particular version of the theory of art for art's sake, a belief that has received unjust criticism within the church and within those artistic communities in which art is believed to have particular uses, either in facilitating worship and devotion or shaping of virtue. For Ortega y Gasset, art appeals to most people if it corresponds most closely to the how they understand reality, if it produces emotions that are familiar, and "succeeds in creating the illusion necessary to make the imaginary personages appear like living persons."[34] Ortega y Gasset regards the conventional approach to art to be merely a form of emotional medication. But he is interested in how art produces other emotions, delves into as-yet-unplumbed depths of experience, and that can only happen through works of art that contradict reality, that detach the viewer from her death grip on practical utility, and render her *passive*.

But this particular kind of aesthetic experience can only happen if art embraces its limits.

> It is not that to any random person of our day art seems less important than it seemed to previous generations, but that the artist himself regards his art as a thing of no consequence. But then again this does not accurately describe the situation. I do not mean to say that the artist makes light of his work and his profession; but they interest him precisely because they are of no transcendent importance.[35]

That modern art—art for art's sake—eschewed transcendence has been almost universally condemned by the church and those committed to art's traditional values as an act of theological violence, an act of nihilistic expression of the death of God. But this is simply not true. The "dehumanization" of modern art is nothing but the recognition of a painting's place in the world: "The trend toward pure art betrays not arrogance, as is often thought, but modesty . . . just art with no other pretenses."[36]

Velázquez and Modern Art

Ortega y Gasset published his provocative analysis and defense of modern art in the very midst of its development in the mid-1920s. Two decades

34. Ibid., 8.
35. Ibid., 49.
36. Ibid., 52.

later, he published several essays on Velázquez, implying that the progenitor of this aesthetic distance is a seventeenth-century court painter who painted portraits, an extraordinarily gifted artist who did not take his gift too seriously, refusing to cling to it as constitutive of his identity.

What artists in the nineteenth and twentieth centuries would develop stylistically, Velázquez seemed to have lived existentially, that is, with a supreme detachment from the pressures and day-to-day battle for mutual recognition that plagues human life, including the world of art. How could a human being so gifted care so little about his gift? Certainly, a human being whose identity is received as grace, whose relationship to God, the world, and himself was not defined by his work as an artist and the paintings he painted. The gifts that Velázquez received from God seemed most gift-like, however, when they were *not* employed, or employed only out of freedom to serve not from personal demand or psychological necessity. He seemed to have preserved God's gifts as gift, as grace. If God had required the return of this gift, Velázquez, I think, would gladly have returned it. Ortega y Gasset's provocative approach to this artist raises the possibility that the seeds of modern art, art for art's sake, and abstraction were sown by a man for whom art was merely the expression of a God-given gift.

But what kind of artist would clean his brush on the canvas he was working on?

An artist that regarded painting as the application of pigment on a scrap of canvas. No more, and no less.

ARTISTS BEHAVING STRANGELY

Why do so many artists behave so strangely? If their odd-looking work isn't enough to make us scratch our heads, their weird behavior confirms our suspicions that they are charlatans, getting away with artistic murder in a laissez-faire and degenerate art world in which personality and image are more important than the quality of their work. No one resembles this portrait of the strangely behaving artist better than Andy Warhol (1928–1987). Everything about him, from his odd appearance, aloof personality, enigmatic statements, and strange collection of friends and associates gives the impression that "Warhol" was a fabrication for media consumption, an act, a ruse. Either he was a creative genius—brilliantly creative beyond our comprehension—or a marketing genius of the P. T. Barnum variety.

But perhaps Warhol's and other artists' strange behavior is due neither to their creative or marketing genius but to a natural human response to a serious problem that all artists, in one way or another, face on a daily basis.

The Anxiety of the Art World

A painting occupies an awkward position in the world. A scrap of canvas with smelly oil paint smeared across it is difficult to justify as useful in this conditional, transactional world. Paintings are thus weak and vulnerable things. Yet vast, complex institutions and networks have emerged to justify them, whether through the auction house (art as priceless luxury item), the museum tour (education), or the local chamber of commerce (art as community service, cultural tourism, or urban revival). That art is ultimately gratuitous creates anxiety and insecurity in the art world. Everyone involved, from art collectors and dealers to critics and curators, has to justify their interest in this seemingly "useless" activity—and justify the money they make or spend on its behalf.

What makes matters worse is that no one knows what makes a great work of art great anyway, or if that work or this work is great. Even the experts are not sure and do not agree. Moreover, the art collectors, the millionaires and billionaires who drive the art world and whose own pursuit of art is itself a powerful form of self-justification, are perhaps the most anxious and most confused of the whole lot. And so collectors must rely on their retinue of dealers, curators, and critics for confirmation. If a collector is going to spend several hundred thousand dollars on pigment smeared on a canvas, she better feel comfortable in her "investment." And so curators, critics, and dealers are desperately looking for markers *other than the painting itself* to assuage the collector's insecurity.

The Artist

Yet for an artist to make a living, these smeared canvases need to be shown, written about, and purchased. In short, these precarious, vulnerable, useless artifacts, which no one is really sure have any "objective" value, or are any good, need to operate as currency in a conditional world, a transactional economy. Yet the work the artist produces operates in direct contradiction to this reality.

Artists feel this precarious situation, even if they are not entirely conscious of it or its origin. It is they who realize, consciously or not, that the works they produce in their studios are vulnerable out in the world, and they who wonder whether the work they do is any good or possesses any lasting value. And this is especially so for those artists whose work is represented by the world's top dealers, shown at the world's most important museums, written about in the world's most important art magazines, and is in the possession of the world's most powerful art collectors. Ironically, I would argue that these are the artists—the ones who work closely with these curators, collectors, dealers, and critics at the highest levels on a daily basis—who feel the insignificance and tenuousness of their work most acutely and the pressure of the conditionality of the art world most strongly because they observe the waves of agendas that may either carry their work to significance or bury it.

Their work needs help to survive. And so many artists cultivate a certain kind of behavior—craft a social role—that simultaneously justifies their work in this context while it protects its integrity, offering a marker for art collectors, curators, dealers, and critics, while releasing artists of the burden of having to explain or defend each work they produce. This is not, however, a new development. It has been a part of the Western artistic tradition since the Renaissance, when painters began to claim that art belonged to the "liberal arts" (philosophy, theology, poetry) and not the "mechanical arts" (trades). The intellectual, the businessman, the scientist, the engineer, the prophet or priest, the entertainer, or the rebel are just a few of the myriad of social roles that artists have adopted throughout the history of art. These roles, which require tremendous effort by artists to develop and maintain, help legitimate the work in what Hegel has called the life-or-death battle for mutual recognition by offering art collectors, curators, and dealers a useful context for appropriating their art for their own purposes.

In this prison house of creative self-expression called the art world, where, following Sartre, everyone is "condemned to freedom," the artist must wear a mask and play a game of high-stakes poker while appearing resistant and transcendent in the face of the contingent, transactional, and conditional nature of the art world.

Yet appearances, as Warhol knew so well, deceive. Behind the aloof, ironic, and "underground" Warhol mask was the weak and vulnerable Andrej Varchola Jr., the Pittsburgh native, the son of a working-class family who emigrated from Slovakia; a lifelong Byzantine Catholic who struggled with his faith in light of his sexual identity; a well-respected commercial designer who became a fine artist *because of his interest in revealing and exploring this Andrej Varchola in his work*; and a devoted friend and selfless promoter of young artists, like Lou Reed and The Velvet Underground. This Andrej Varchola miraculously survived an attempted murder in 1968—a gunshot wound to the chest—the physical and psychological effects of which he struggled with the remainder of his life, "gnawed within and scorched without," as Melville describes Ahab in *Moby-Dick*. Warhol's work, like his life, revealed the constant presence and judgment of death lurking around every corner in a culture that idolized youth, fame, and freedom. Warhol/

Varchola died of cardiac arrest in 1986 after a routine gall bladder surgery, a surgery he put off because of his fear of doctors and hospitals after the trauma of his gunshot wound.

Warhol, You, and Me

Warhol was a lot like you and me—only more so. He was neither a genius nor a fake. He was profoundly, utterly human, justifying his work and his existence through the means available to him, and deeply insecure about its value in one of our culture's most fickle, unpredictable, and insecure institutions: the contemporary art world.

So, when you are tempted to dismiss the contemporary art world as irrelevant because of the strange behavior of its artists, remember that their behavior is an admission that their work—what they spend their lives making and to which they are profoundly devoted and committed—is weak and vulnerable. And their personas are not only masks, but also the armor and weaponry that they are using in this suffocating art world.

What masks do we wear, what armor do we put on, what social roles do we craft, and what strange behavior do we cultivate to justify our own weak and vulnerable work, or perhaps allow it to address our audience in as effective a way as possible?

DAMIEN HIRST IS FREE

The market for artist Damien Hirst's work seems to have bottomed out.[37] And those who find his stuffed sharks, bejeweled skulls, and dot paintings overhyped and unjustifiable are delighted. The invisible hand of the art market has finally pulled back the curtain, they will say, revealing Hirst to be the sham they all thought he was in the first place. I admire Hirst's work and feel that it possesses an unusual aesthetic and theological depth that is often overlooked by both his supporters and detractors. And it was precisely for the sake of this overlooked aesthetic and theological depth that I was delighted to learn of Hirst's failure.

The art market—manifest at auction—gauges demand and desire at a particular moment and as such it is an important tool for the determination of an artist's current value. Yet its influence has significant limits, for it cannot establish (or maintain) the aesthetic value of an artist's work over the broad arc of a decades-long career. It cannot in large part because collectors,

---

37. Rice, "Damien Hirst."

who, with their dealers and advisors, drive the market, are in the business of collecting art. They are collecting desire and demand, values that are not aesthetic but economic. Many of the most well-known artists of the Western tradition go in and out of favor at auction even long after their death.

Most collectors speculate. They buy art to acquire cultural capital and sell at a profit. They are constantly on the lookout for young, "emerging" artists in which they can invest, which means that they acquire several works for several thousand dollars, which encourages (i.e., pressures) their collector friends (i.e., rivals or disciples) to follow suit. With their dealers and a train of museum curators, these collectors work to create value and maintain scarcity. Several high-profile museum exhibitions and some scholarly work on the artist's art historical importance later, the influential collector will begin to sell the work at auction, hopefully at a large profit, or gift artwork to museums, which offer intangible profits that only cultural benefactors can earn.

The artist's value is determined not by how much a collector paid for the work at a gallery that represents the artist, but how much the collector is able to sell it for, usually at auction. This is the secondary market. Everyone involved—artists, dealers, collectors—knows this, and they work hard to manage the auctions, which are gracefully choreographed theatrical performances that hide the bloody and brutal fight club of the secondary market. The market was an inaccurate gauge to justify Hirst's value when he was hot. And it is just as inaccurate now that he is not.

Andy Warhol famously said that in the future everyone will be famous for fifteen minutes. Hirst seems to know that his are approaching their end. And this is not such a bad thing as he enters into his most creatively productive years, the years of an artist's life with which collectors and dealers historically have had such notorious difficulty. I admire Hirst's commitment to his studio practice, and I find much of his work aesthetically and theologically profound, in large part because of his deceptive focus on death, but it was too easily lost amidst the accouterments of his notorious celebrity.

His art market failure has freed Hirst from a twenty-five-year sentence as an art world "provocateur," a fashionable bête noir, and all of the pressure that comes with trying to maintain his work's value through it. If he chooses to accept his parole and embrace his freedom, Hirst might get down to the business of producing work that explores emotional and existential territory which his work to this point has only offered passing glances at.

This "failure" might give his work enough space to be reconsidered by curators and critics, allowing them to dig deeper into his work without the market pressures that lurk over those artists in fashion and to discern how and in what ways Hirst's work receives and passes on the living tradition of artistic practice. Born in 1965, Hirst is only just now entering his most richly productive years as an artist. And so his art world failure just might be the best thing that ever happened to him as a human being. And that can only benefit his art.

5

THE ART

The painter no longer approached his easel with an image in his mind; he went up to it with material in his hand to do something to that other piece of material in front of him. The image would be the result of this encounter.

—HAROLD ROSENBERG, "THE AMERICAN ACTION PAINTERS"

I am for an art that embroils itself with the everyday crap
& still comes out on top.

—CLAES OLDENBURG

JOUSTING THE QUINCE TREE: REALISM AND PAINTING

Let's face it: the world doesn't interest us much. It's just there, as a backdrop. It is visual background noise onto which we lay our own emotional tracks. We are too busy, as David Foster Wallace once put it, "ruling our little skull-sized kingdoms" to notice the way the late-afternoon light hits this tree, or that brilliantly colored finch, or that toddler with his mother. Ask us what visual experiences stood out for us on any single day, and we would be hard-pressed to recall *anything*.

And yet, for some reason, we demand that our paintings be "realistic," that is, that they offer recognizable and familiar imagery. We demand visual imagery that conforms to our (distracted) recollections of what we think "reality" is, even though we spend so little time actually looking at the world around us. We want art to comfort us, to serve our needs, to add a little visual seasoning (but not too much) to the gray world in which we live out our daily lives. (This is even the case for those of us who are fond of talking about the goodness of the physical world.) Perhaps we go even further and claim to affirm and celebrate this world as God's good creation, but have we ever spent five minutes looking at the stem of a rose or the deep red of a pomegranate?

We want our artists to keep us distracted by producing images that reaffirm our disenchanted, ironic, and pragmatic view of the world. Give us stuff we "know," imagery that conforms to how we already use the world. We want art to tell us we're "right"—right about our presumptions about how the world works. The Getty Research Center in Los Angeles has discovered that we spend an average of thirty seconds looking at a painting. Thirty seconds? However, for what we usually want from it, perhaps thirty seconds is more than enough.

This is often what we mean when we claim to like our art "realistic." *But it is not realism.* It a delusion, a reflection of our unwillingness to see in nature or the world more than merely convenient tools for our physical or emotional use.

Realism

Realism in the visual arts was a nineteenth-century reaction to the excessive idealism cultivated by the official academic art establishment, of which such artists as William-Adolphe Bourguereau (1825–1905), Alexandre Cabanel (1823–1899), and Jean-Léon Gérome (1824–1904) were the most well-known practitioners. They sought to "perfect" nature, to present, as academic painter Thomas Couture observed about Raphael, whom the academy claimed to emulate:

> Everything in his pictures is represented in the springtime of life; men, women, flowers; all are young; elegance, gracefulness, purity, simplicity of lines . . . here is life without its wear."[1]

1. Quoted in Nochlin, ed., *Realism and Tradition in Art 1848–1900*, 6.

It was against the repetition of artistic conventions rather than the close observation of the world that the realists, chief among them Gustave Courbet, rebelled. For Courbet, it was neither literature nor other works of art but nature that was the artist's model: "The beauty provided by nature is superior to all the conventions of the artist."[2] Moreover, Courbet reacted vociferously against the excessive use of mythological and literary themes with no connection to lived experience. What was Courbet's response to the narcotic of idealism and mythology? He proposed a radical aesthetic detox that reorientated painting toward the observable, creaturely world: "The art of painting can only consist of the representation of objects which are visible and tangible for the artist."[3] Asked about why he did not paint angels, Courbet's infamous response was, "Show me an angel and I will paint it."

Let's look more closely at a contemporary artist working in the wake of Courbet's radical vision for art.

A Contemporary Realist

For the Spanish painter Antonio López García (born 1936), the world glows with the aura of enchantment and crackles with wonder. A 2011 monograph on the artist chronicles his sixty-year career, a career about which I knew little before encountering this beautifully illustrated and informative publication.[4] López García's work is not well known outside Spain, and progressive critics have too easily dismissed it as "academic." Although he is deeply concerned with preserving technique and craft, he is not an idealist. His life has been singularly devoted to grappling with nature, with what he sees of the world around him. But he is concerned not merely with what he sees but with what he *feels* when he sees.

López García was born in Tomelloso, Ciudad Real, in central Spain, a part of the plain of La Mancha made famous by Miguel de Cervantes in *Don Quixote*. He moved to Madrid in 1949 to study at the Escuela de Bellas Artes de San Fernando, where he finished in 1955. He had his first solo exhibition in Madrid in 1957 and soon became the leader of the Madrid Realists, a group of artists who sought to revitalize academic painting and figuration. In the 1960s, his reputation began to grow outside Spain with exhibitions in Paris and New York, and he has enjoyed international acclaim since. The Museum of Fine Arts in Boston hosted a solo exhibition of his work in 2008, and three years later, the Museo Thyssen-Bornemisza in Madrid organized

2. Quoted in ibid., 35.
3. Quoted in ibid.
4. Serraller and Delibes, *Antonio López García*.

a retrospective exhibition, establishing him, along with abstract sculpture Eduardo Chillida and abstract painter Antoni Tàpies, as one of the most important Spanish artists of the postwar generation.

López García paints portraits, landscapes, and still lifes, focusing on the humble environs of the periphery of Madrid, where the "old way" lingers. To many in the art world, raised on the immediate rush and shocking jolt of the avant-garde, his quiet, painstaking works appear naïve and old-fashioned, irrelevant to the demands of contemporary life. And viewed among the stuffed sharks, stainless-steel bunny rabbits, and Japanese anime that feature so prominently in contemporary art, López García is an anachronism, an aesthetic Don Quixote, an artist who still believes that painting is magical, mysterious, and perhaps even a little heroic.

Two great predecessors who have been helpful in López García's quest are the Italian Renaissance painter Piero della Francesca (1415–1492) and the Spanish Baroque painter Diego Velázquez (1599–1660). As a student, López García admired and came to emulate Piero's monumental stillness, the quiet, geometric, and even sculptural nature of his compositions. But ironically, it was not until he was in Italy in 1955 that he discovered the simplicity and grace of Spanish art, especially that of Velázquez.

A painter does not paint what he knows but paints in order to know, to discover something about himself and the world. For López García, the process of painting is a struggle, a knock-down–drag-out brawl with the world, which refuses to yield its secrets or give a blessing too easily. He is notorious for working methodically and meticulously, which has limited his production and, consequently, the opportunities he has had to show his work, averaging only around two solo exhibitions *per decade*. In an art world in which artists generate multiple exhibitions each year and whose studios resemble factories, it is refreshing that he approaches the production of each artifact, whether a painting or sculpture, with the focus and intentionality of a priest performing a sacrament.

For most of us, the world is no longer a cause of fascination, of sustained contemplation and reflection. A bird is just a bird, a vase of flowers just that, and the grace of this man or the charm of that woman is buried beneath a multitude of judgments we make about them as they pass us. *This* is the "real world," the world in which, as Cervantes once wrote, an inn is just an inn.

But López García, by looking closely and observing intently, paints the inn as if it were a castle, investing such prosaic, overlooked, and insignificant subjects as a bowl of fruit, dirty laundry soaking in a pan, a bathroom, a skinned rabbit, a refrigerator, and a woman in a bathtub with a dignity that is, quite frankly, disturbing. López García makes paintings that are the result of his struggle with objects and experiences we rarely ever notice, much less take seriously as worth our visual recognition and contemplation.

A Quince Tree

One of the more remarkable and stubbornly beautiful and seductive objects in the world for López García is the quince tree in his backyard. For decades he has tried to paint this simple tree as it absorbs and refracts sunlight. In 1992, filmmaker Victor Erice was given unique access to the artist's world to make the award-winning documentary *El Sol del Membrillo* (*The Quince Tree of the Sun*). The film tells the story of López García's approach to art through his relationship with this little tree, which he feels the urge to paint every autumn. And yet every autumn it thwarts his attempt to capture his experience of it. To watch the artist around this tree offers a rare and revealing insight into the mystery of artistic practice, of smearing paint on a scrap of canvas, and the naïve yet powerfully sophisticated attention of a man fascinated with nature, a man whose paintings reveal nature not only to be beautiful, but to be something more, a mysterious and inexplicable gift.

Realism and Abstraction

In the nineteenth century, Realism redirected the artist to the world—to culture as well as nature. Interestingly, when the artist's gaze was turned toward the world, toward its close observation, that gaze initiated the developments that led to abstraction. Far from being the result of turning away from the world, "modern art" is the aesthetic tradition par excellence of a turn toward the world. In his book, *Modern Art and the Death of a Culture* (1970), art historian and evangelical statesman H. R. Rookmaaker was right to locate the demise of "Art" with Courbet's realism. But he was wrong, I would suggest, to lament it.

Realism, as well as the tradition of modern art that Courbet initiated, discloses the awe-inspiring beauty as well as the heartbreaking injustice in the world. Those who want art only to make them feel good about their beliefs or distract them from the pressures of the day shouldn't demand that their art be "realistic." And under no circumstances should they look at the painting and sculpture of Antonio López García.

PISS CHRIST REVISITED

Not long ago I presented an image of Andres Serrano's infamous photograph, entitled *Piss Christ* (1987), for discussion to a class of seminary students. From a series of photographs Serrano made between 1987–90, entitled *Immersions*, this photograph became an icon for the bloody culture wars of the early 1990s. My students were shocked by the image. Not because it was blasphemous or vulgar, but because the work so clearly contradicted the image in their imagination, which had been produced by descriptions of the work in the news media over the last two decades. Although most of the students knew *of* the controversial work, few had actually *seen* an image of it. They knew it as pundits, journalists, and commentators described it: "a crucifix submerged in a jar of the artist's urine." In fact, several of the students were convinced that there was "another" *Piss Christ*, one that more accurately fit the description. I was an undergraduate studying modern and contemporary art when the controversy exploded and I still have the image in my mind that the words of the title produced, an image that was *Piss Christ* until I saw it in person several years later.

Works of visual art—paintings, photographs, video, sculpture, drawings—are vulnerable artifacts in large part because they are inextricably enmeshed in language, from which they emerge and also quickly return. And so no work of art is, or can be, a "purely" visual experience. The fact that there was no "other" *Piss Christ*, one more offensive—one more clearly anti-Christian, one less *beautiful*, one that fits the terse vulgarity of its description—reveals the power of words to shape our experience, including our experience of the visual arts.

Another challenge that faces the work of art is that we are often first introduced to the visual arts through journalism, through the transmission of news and current events, through descriptions, or as "images" that are intended to serve to illustrate political or cultural issues. Moreover, most works of art that enter into the media do so as spectacle or controversy. Rarely do we encounter works of art as the artist intends them to be experienced, which is to stand in front of them in a gallery or museum, to allow them to address us as viewers, and, perhaps most importantly, viewers who are receptive to such an experience of being addressed aesthetically. This is an experience that cannot be reduced to an "idea" or a "meaning" or a "world view," but lives in and through the viewer's personal response to being addressed by the works of art.

Given the fact the *Piss Christ* was taken from its intended viewership in the art world in order to function in a broader media context, it is not surprising that politically conservative North American Christians—Catholic,

Protestant, and Evangelical—presume that Andres Serrano is an anti-Christian artist whose work is intended to impugn the Christian tradition, revealing the latent atheism of the contemporary art world as a whole.

Although the controversy erupted over twenty years ago, it remains part of the folklore of cultural politics that continues to underwrite Christian witness in the public arena. In April 2011, in Avignon, France, four young men attacked *Piss Christ* while it was on public view, and in October 2012 Edward Tyler Nahem Fine Art in New York presented "Body and Spirit: Andres Serrano 1987–2012," a retrospective exhibition of Serrano's work that included *Piss Christ*. Curated by Walter Robinson, former editor of *Artnet.com* magazine, the exhibition was on view on the eve of the presidential election, which some cultural warriors, like Bill Donohue, president of New York's Catholic League, claimed was an orchestrated effort to undermine Western culture and Christianity.[5] And so it appears that Serrano's *Piss Christ* continues to serve as an icon for a culture war that right-wing Christians refuse to believe was lost at the outset and a war that now seems to be fought not in the political but cultural arenas. Accordingly, it is perhaps more relevant than ever to revisit this deeply misunderstood photograph.

The Controversy

Serrano (born 1950) had received $15,000 from the Southeastern Center for Contemporary Art (SECCA) in Winston-Salem, North Carolina in 1988, to produce work that would be exhibited, with the work of nine other artists. The exhibition traveled to Los Angeles, Pittsburgh, and Richmond with no controversy. After the tour had ended, the American Family Association, an activist organization founded by Rev. Donald Wildmon, denounced Serrano and initiated a letter-writing campaign to both houses of Congress that spurred Senator Jesse Helms on his crusade against the National Endowment for the Arts (NEA) in order to prevent funding to artists whose work is determined to be obscene or denigrates religious belief.[6]

The Photograph

Politicians and media pundits described *Piss Christ* as "a plastic crucifix submerged in the artist's own urine." But the image that this description conjures bears almost no relationship to the reality of the work itself, which

5. Quoted in Boucher, "Andres Serrano *Piss Christ* Still Pissing Off Christians."

6. Niederkorn, "The Man Behind A Controversy Andres Serrano . . ."

stands five feet high and over three feet long, and features a crucifix captured above eye-level, glowing with a deep orange and yellow light that "looks like a giant still picture from a religious film, with Jesus on the cross bathed in divine light and brilliant color."[7]

Serrano achieves this dramatic effect by photographing the crucifix through a Plexiglas container filled with urine, hence the rather prosaic title, a title that indicates that the artist "want[s] people to know what they're looking at. I realized (the title) would be ambiguously provocative, but I just didn't have a problem with that at all."[8]

Since 1983, Serrano's work has been characterized by the creation of beautiful images of the most repugnant and taboo subjects, such as cadavers, mutilated animals, the homeless, and even high-ranking members of the Ku Klux Klan. Serrano's work creates a virtually inexplicable experience, in which horror is overwhelmed in and through beauty. The horror does not disappear—the tragedy of the suicide in the morgue, the severed cow's head, or the racism of the Klan member remain—but is received through beauty. Serrano's is an aesthetic vision that sees beauty in not merely a "broken" world, as we are fond of saying, but in a world that is torn asunder in horror (suicides and lynchings), in which even the food that we eat demands savage butchery.

It is also the world of bodily fluids, such as blood, milk, semen, urine, and feces, which disgust us but are the very means by which our lives emerge and are sustained. And Serrano uses these disgusting yet life-giving fluids as aesthetic media. He observes, "Visually, the bodily fluids worked for me beautifully. . . . They gave me the colors that I was looking for, the light."[9]

In a remarkable poem based on *Piss Christ*, the poet Andrew Hudgins writes:

> We are born between the urine and the feces, Augustine says,
> and so was Christ, if there was a Christ, skidding into this world
> as we do on a tide of blood and urine. Blood, feces, urine— what
> the fallen world is made of, and what we make.[10]

Hudgins's poem reveals the deeply Christian intuition of *Piss Christ*. According to Rowan Williams, "The goal of the Christian life becomes not enlightenment but wholeness—acceptance of this complicated and muddled

7. Ibid.
8. Ibid.
9. Ibid.
10. Hudgins, "Piss Christ."

bundle of experiences as the possible theater for God's work."[11] And Serrano's work in general and *Piss Christ* in particular, if it does not quite understand it theologically, feels this acceptance aesthetically.

The Artist

Born in Cuba and raised a Catholic, Serrano has observed in a recent video interview: "Although I don't consider myself a Catholic, I see myself as a Christian." Therefore, far from being an outsider denigrating Christianity, Serrano operates as an insider, although, at his admission, not a traditional one. And so, "As a Christian I had the right to use the symbols of the church." In addition, he is very aware of the diversity within the tradition of Christian art: "There is a tradition of a bizarre and very strange spirituality connected with Catholicism and Christianity."[12] Serrano is a serious collector of religious art, especially medieval sculpture and furniture, and a lover of European churches. And perhaps just as surprising to those who regard him as an art world agitator and provocateur, Serrano describes himself as a traditional and classical artist. And indeed, influenced as he is by the Spanish tradition, including Goya, El Greco, and the filmmaking of Luis Buñuel, his photographs suggest a deeply Spanish classicism and religious focus.

But although his work is formed by a Christian vision and emerges from his own appropriation of Christian belief, Serrano makes his photographs to create an experience *for the viewer*. The "meaning" of his work is not circumscribed by his intentions, his beliefs, but exists, as T. S. Eliot said, "between the reader and the poem."

> In a sense, my work has always been like a mirror. Whoever looks at it will have a different reaction, and they'll get it from what they give, and if they give it a negative energy that's what they'll get back, whereas if you give it a positive energy you'll get back a positive image, a reaffirmation rather than a negation.[13]

"He is not an artist, he is a jerk."

But *Piss Christ* was not allowed to become a mirror for self-reflection in the hands of the politicians and culture warriors. Nor was it allowed to exist as

11. Williams, *The Wound of Knowledge*, 12.
12. Niederkorn, "The Man Behind a Controversy Andres Serrano . . ."
13. Ibid.

a beautiful artifact, or create an experience that deepens our experience as human beings, or, in fact, to become a means of grace, of God's love in the midst of death, darkness, and evil. In fact, understanding *Piss Christ* or hearing from the artist who made it seemed to be of no concern. It was merely an "image" that could be used to score political victories. Jesse Helms, the one who championed Christian values, even said about Serrano, "I hope I never meet him. He is not an artist, he is a jerk."[14]

In the public arena *Piss Christ* did not even exist as an image; it was deprived of its integrity as a visual work and existed only as a description, "a crucifix submerged in the artist's urine." Over time, this phrase became a performative speech act, creating the emotional anxiety that the political Right could use to win political battles. (I was an undergraduate art history major at the time and had heard this phrase repeated ad nauseam by politicians and commentators, from Rush Limbaugh and Bill Bennett to George Will. Yet when I actually saw the photograph in person, I was stunned by the disparity between the image that had existed in my imagination and the photograph that confronted me.)

And yet for Serrano, negative responses to his work were accepted—that is, if those responses emerge from an encounter with the work of art itself.

> Even though this overreaction caused me a great deal of distress
> . . . the one thing I've never tried to do is to manipulate the audience's reaction. I can't fault people with their interpretations, because if that's what they see, then it's valid for them, and I intend the work to be open-ended.[15]

Iconoclasm and Iconoclasts

But it is this very open-endedness, the agency of an artifact as it speaks, and does so not with a single "meaning" but in connection with a viewer and her own (not the artist's) cauldron of feelings that simmer just below the conscious surface—it is this open-endedness that can give *Piss Christ* its power. It draws to the surface our ambivalences, our emotional conflicts, our pain. And that has elicited, and continues to elicit, violence. In April 2011, in Avignon, France, four young men attacked it while it was on public view. As is often the case, iconoclasm—the destruction of images—reveals not only the power of imagery, but suggests that the iconoclasts hold to an exaggerated or misplaced power, imbuing the artifact with more influence,

14. Ibid.
15. Ibid.

more communicative power, than it actually possesses.[16] And for Serrano, he recognizes that he works with symbols and representations.

> What the nuns told us . . . was that we worship not the crucifix but Christ. . . .We weren't supposed to worship the symbol or give it the same level of reverence that we give Christ, because it's only a representation. It's just a symbol.[17]

It seems that it is Serrano, not the right-wing political activists claiming to preserve traditional values, who seem to misunderstand the distinction between God and the creation, between the creator and the creature.

A Theology of Glory

Sociologist James Davison Hunter has demonstrated that the culture wars have been conducted through a theology of glory, that is, a theology that has identified God's work with worldly success: with winning elections, raising money, achieving influence, increasing strength, defeating the enemy.[18] A theology of glory is a theology that glorifies the power of politics and instrumentalizes other practices, like the arts—considering them to be of value only as a means toward achieving political ends.

Yet the case of *Piss Christ* reveals just how difficult it is to control modern and contemporary art and to make it serve as an ideological weapon in the culture wars. *Piss Christ* also reveals that, in sharp contrast to a theology of glory, modern and contemporary art operates in a register that Luther would call a theology of the cross—a theology that experiences God in the suffering, evil, and ugliness that form each individual life experience. *Piss Christ* is a work that connects to our belief and doubt, fear and confidence, pain and exhilaration, of honest confession of weakness. And it is in that space that this maligned photograph creates that God's grace can be felt. For what is the cross but the reality of, as Hudgins writes, "God thrown in human waste, submerged and shining."[19] Serrano observed that in the end, his intention with the photograph was "to aestheticize Christ."

To do so with piss—that is grace.

16. See Siedell, "Icons and Iconoclasm," 108–15.
17. Niederkorn, "The Man Behind a Controversy Andres Serrano . . ."
18. See Hunter, *Culture Wars* and *To Change the World*.
19. Hudgins, "Piss Christ."

"I LOVE THE EARTH"—TARKOVSKY'S *ANDREI RUBLEV*

For me, the sky is empty.

—ANDREI TARKOVSKY

A great work of art continues to work long after the initial encounter. It seems to metastasize, spreading throughout your imaginative life, burrowing into all of the crevices of your emotional and intellectual life—especially those new ideas and experiences that remain raw and unassimilated. This has been my experience with Andrei Tarkovsky's *The Passion According To Andrei* (1966), a film that was recommended to me over ten years ago on two separate occasions by two different people I deeply respect, a Cuban artist living in Los Angeles and a German curator living in New York City.

The film neither spurred me to devour Tarkovsky's other works nor to become an accomplished student of the history of modern film and cinema. In fact, it seems to have prevented me from conceiving of it merely as an *introduction* to Tarkovsky or the genre. This single film, perhaps because of its cosmic scope and psychological intimacy, seems strangely sufficient as a cinematic framework for my life. I can only confess that *The Passion According to Andrei* is simply not finished with me yet, and apparently, neither am I with it. For some reason, my friends knew that in it was something for which I yearned. And ten years later, that yearning seems not to have abated.

A Painting

"*The Trinity* that can be found in the Tretjakov gallery in Moscow gave me the idea for the film. Upon seeing the icon I was able to imagine life in this terrible time."[20] Tarkovsky's experience of a single painting, Andrei Rublev's famous icon *The Holy Trinity* (c. 1455), was the origin of his second feature film, which focused on the famous Russian icon painter, of whose life virtually nothing is known. The film is about a painting, although Rublev is never depicted painting the picture and in fact the film depicts the time before he decides to paint the picture and culminates only in the monk's decision to go to Moscow to paint it.

---

20. Tarkovsky, *Sculpting in Time*, 5.

What interested Tarkovsky about Rublev and his icon *The Holy Trinity* were the conditions out of which it was created. How can such artistic beauty come from such inhumane suffering? Tarkovsky explains, "At a time when the life of the people was hopeless, when they were oppressed by a foreign yoke, by injustice, by poverty, Rublev expressed in his art a hope, a faith in the future."[21] For Tarkovsky, "He strove to express an all-embracing harmony of the world, the serenity of the soul."[22] Tarkovsky continues, "In spite of seeing and perceiving this universe with great pain . . . Rublev goes further. He doesn't express the unbearable weight of his life, of the world around him. He looks for the grain of hope, of love, of faith among the people of his time."[23]

Tarkovsky's goal was not to make a biography, but to use a historical figure in order to explore the "difficulty of being an artist."[24] Tarkovsky continued, "We worked at drowning our idea in the atmosphere, in the characters, in the conflicts between the characters."[25] The result was a two-and-a-half-hour film made up of six black-and-white vignettes, some which do not even include Rublev, which paint a bleak emotional landscape of inescapable suffering through bitter cold, snow, mud, poverty, and indescribable cruelty, within and against which the artist struggled.

Rublev and Boriska

Against this backdrop of misery, the pursuit of art seems at best gratuitous and at worst evil—a retreat from the harsh realities of public life into the comfortable confines of the private imagination. Tarkovsky narrates Rublev's struggle with his vocation, which includes a spiritual crisis, brought on by a call from the Trinity Lavra of St. Sergius outside of Moscow, the spiritual center of the Russian Orthodox Church, to paint an icon of the Trinity. Rublev resists. And he doubts. He also refuses to paint a Final Judgment painting because he refuses to fill the townspeople with terror. He cannot reconcile the love of God with the evil and brutality that he has observed in the world and in his heart. (He had also killed a man during the sack of Vladimir.) He believes that he is unworthy to fulfill such an important spiritual commission. And Rublev struggles with the futility of art in the face of such suffering, beauty in the face of evil—including his own.

21. Ibid., 14.
22. Ibid., 15.
23. Ibid., 22.
24. Ibid., 21.
25. Ibid., 18.

And so he fasts.

He fasts from speaking. He fasts from community. And he fasts from his vocation. Never does the viewer see Rublev with a paintbrush in his hand.

As he wanders the Russian countryside wrestling with his disbelief through the practice of an austere Christian asceticism, he discovers the sensual earthly beauty of pagan rites. He then comes upon a young boy, Boriska, who is involved in another kind of vocational struggle. His father, a bell maker, has just died, forcing upon the boy the responsibility of finishing the casting of a bell for a village church. (The icon and the bell are crucial for Russian Orthodox theology and worship—the icon reveals the world transformed visually by grace, and the bell is the merciful voice of God, which calls all to follow him.) The boy, desperate to achieve recognition from the townspeople and the prince who commissioned the bell, risks his life by claiming to have been given the secret of bell casting by his father. Unlike Rublev, who refuses to paint, the boy risks his life to create beauty, doing so out of the mud and clay, tension and anger of the townspeople, and his own fear, because his father has not passed the secret of bell casting on to him. (We also learn that because of the cost of the project, if Boriska fails, the prince will kill him.)

Rublev watches the boy from a distance in silence. He watches Boriska pretend to know what he's doing—and yet he is merely imitating what he has observed his father do. But Boriska's desperate improvisation is successful. He casts the bell for the village and saves his life in the process. But he collapses from exhaustion, grief, and anguish. His father has taken the secrets of bell making to his grave, leaving the young boy alone—a son with no father, a bell maker with no knowledge.

Breaking his fast from speech to comfort the suffering boy who is laying in the mud, Rublev then vows to break another fast: "We will go to the Trinity Monastery, and you will make bells and I will paint icons." The film leaves unsaid the particular reason of Rublev's decision to go to Moscow, fulfill his commission, and return to his vocation. But the answer is inseparable from the young boy's suffering, his willingness to risk everything for his art, and the compassion Rublev has for him.

The answer is found in the relationship between a suffering boy, an unknown youth who faked it and succeeded in making art, and the other, a well-known painter who has refused to succeed by not painting pictures. Yet against the crushing desolation and loneliness that both feel and with all evidence to the contrary, Rublev resolves not to give up. Rublev returns to his vocation, clings to what God has given and gifted him to do—not in triumph, but in humble obedience. He will simply fulfill the commissions at a church that awaits his gifts, a church that *needs* what God has gifted him to make. And Rublev will bring Boriska with him, so that he may exercise his own gift, live into a vocation he does not yet realize he already possesses. One of the paintings Rublev will paint is the icon of the Holy Trinity, arguably the most well-known icon ever painted, and a painting that will be the reason the monk was made a saint in the Russian Orthodox Church in 1988.

Loving Your Neighbor

Tarkovsky's Rublev recovers his vocation not in an act of proving his love for God, but as an act of love for his neighbor, which is a result of his faith—by comforting Boriska and offering him the opportunity to accompany the well-known painter. Rublev becomes, in effect, his father, his mentor, and his patron, creating space for the boy to practice his art form. The battle that Rublev fights throughout the film is indeed with God and his troubled conscience—the spiritual responsibility of painting icons is too great in the face of his doubts, and the pain and suffering around him make his talent and the fame he has acquired irrelevant. And yet Boriska's suffering and the comfort that Rublev offers him seem to liberate the painter from that heavy burden of a spiritual offering to God, of justifying himself (and his faith) before God through his artistic work, an obligation that had become impossible for him. Forsaking his artistic vocation before God, Rublev rediscovers it through his suffering neighbor, finding it in the mud and sorrow.

There is a tendency inside and outside the church to overspiritualize art, to regard it as a means of redemption or an indication of spiritual strength. And this is especially so in the ascetic tradition of the Russian Orthodox Church, which forms the religious backdrop of *Andrei Rublev*. And yet Tarkovsky's cinematic vision is of the earth. Rublev recovers his vocation by reconnecting with the material simplicity of "painting icons and making bells." Artifacts that come from the dirt and mud are thus returned to the world.

Surprisingly, the Protestant Reformer Martin Luther's understanding of vocation is helpful. The God who justifies sinful human beings through faith redirects our work—whether paintings icons, casting bells, or coaching a high school football team—from pleasing God to serving our neighbor. The beneficiary of our work is thus not God but our neighbor. Our work is a means by which God is at work in the world.

Mud

The film begins with an unusual prologue, called "Flying," in which a man, reminiscent of Icarus, builds a hot air balloon and attempts to fly. The exhilaration of the flight is brief, as the man crashes and dies in the mud, is returned to the earth. And it is the earth that is the focus of the film, the focus of Rublev's spiritual journey. Tarkovsky explains, "What interests me at all times, and most of all, is precisely the earth."[26] Again, it is the German Reformer's earthiness that Tarkovsky's aesthetic recalls. In response to those whose spirituality finds them ascending the heavens, Luther responds somewhere that God is not there. God, in the person of Christ, is here, in our suffering, in the mud and mire. "I never see the mud," Tarkovsky continues, "I only see the earth mixed with water, the mire from which things grow. I love the earth. I love my earth."[27] It is the crashing to the mud that brings death to the mysterious man who flies and it is the mud that is the source of new life for Rublev and Boriska, both of whom take the dirt and clay and make from it their icons and bells.

The Holy Trinity

In the last few minutes of the film, black-and-white film imagery gives way to an explosion of color, in which the camera offers close-up details of Rublev's brilliantly colored icons, culminating in the famous *Holy Trinity*. Rublev transforms the dirt into the brilliant pigments that preach Christ to the faithful, a promise of hope, a promise that every tear will be wiped away, everything sad will be made untrue, a promise of harmony out of the chaos. Tarkovsky's film poses the question, how can such a masterpiece of art and beauty emerge from such pain and suffering? Tarkovsky observes, "Art is born and takes hold wherever there is a timeless and insatiable longing for the spiritual, for the ideal: that longing that draws people to art."[28] The answer, which the film seems to offer in and through the mud, is grace.

26. Ibid., 25.
27. Ibid., 26.
28. Ibid., 38.

RUBLEV'S *HOLY TRINITY*: A PROMISE IN PAINT

"There exists the icon of the Trinity by St. Andrei Rublev; therefore God exists."

This statement by Father Pavel Florensky, Russian Orthodox priest, mathematician, art historian, and martyr, is not the kind of apologetic strategy that Christians in the West are used to. To Western ears, Florensky lacks objectivity and intellectual rigor. His statement sounds woolly, mystical, and irrational. This is not simply because we have inherited a different apologetics; we also have inherited a very different aesthetics.

In the Western tradition, we tend to view art as something that should depict the world around us, express our emotions, and teach moral or ethical truths. In short, it *represents*—sometimes the visible world of things, sometimes the abstract world of ideas or the inner world of emotions. And therefore it tends to play a subservient (i.e., decorative) role in the production of knowledge or truth. At its best art can only illustrate truth, help us "visualize" it by wrapping it in attractive garments. But at its worst it is an idolatrous distraction. The result is that Western viewers and critics both inside and outside the church tend to consider works of art to be texts, visual illustrations of a philosophical truth or a theological world view that need to be "read." As a museum curator for over a decade, I can attest to this tendency among audiences, whether young or old, novice or expert, to see art's value as the occasion to talk about something else, something more important. Art must know its place in the Western epistemological line.

The Icon

Yet in the Eastern church this is not so. Art does something else. The place to begin to unpack this distinctive approach is with Florensky's own example, *The Holy Trinity* painted by the Russian monk Andrei Rublev (1370-c.1430), which depicts three seemingly identical persons sitting around a table, persons that have traditionally been interpreted as the Father, Son, and Holy Spirit. St. Vladimir's Seminary Press has published the first English translation of an insightful, profound, yet comprehensible introduction to this most famous of icons. Originally written in German in 1994 by the Benedictine eremitical monk Gabriel Bunge, *The Rublev Trinity* has been translated into English by Andrew Louth, well-known scholar of the Fathers of the Eastern Orthodox Church.[29]

29. Bunge, *The Rublev Trinity*. Subsequent references to this book are indicated parenthetically in the text.

What little is known of Andrei Rublev comes from *The Life of St. Nikon of Radonezh*, a hagiography of Rublev's spiritual father compiled by a Serbian monk who also wrote the hagiography of St. Sergii of Radonezh (1314–1392), the spiritual father of Nikon often called the "Abbot of Russia." (The fact that so little is known about Rublev's life gave Tarkovsky the freedom he needed to invent it in film.) Venerated as a saint even during his lifetime, St. Sergii's spiritual life was intimately related to the *mysterium Trinitatis*. Bunge shows how Rublev's spiritual life, through Sergii and Nikon, was shaped by a particular devotion to the Trinity, and Rublev's icon emerges from this distinctive spiritual formation.

The monk's practice as an icon painter is inseparable from his practice as a Christian. The icon is thus more than theology in paint. It is prayer in paint. This achievement was only possible through the ascetical disciplines. Rublev and his friend and "fellow faster" Daniil, himself an accomplished icon painter, would sit for hours simply contemplating an icon of the Holy Trinity in St. Sergii's Trinity Monastery. Bunge demonstrates that it is this devotion that nourished Rublev's soul and prepared him for his greatest aesthetic achievement.

Needless to say, Rublev was not the first to paint an icon of the Trinity. There is a long and diverse history of images relating to the mysterious scene of Genesis 18, in which three visitors, commonly interpreted by Christian readers to be the triune God, announce to Abraham and Sarah that they would have a son, Isaac, who will become the child of promise. Bunge discerns three different but closely related iconographic traditions preceding Rublev, and he explores how he assimilated aspects of each while he simultaneously and ingeniously innovated new forms in such a manner that it was "thoroughly traditional and, equally in an unqualified sense, unique" (13).

Rublev's challenge was to "give each particular figure an unmistakable countenance" (89). Following the distinctions of Gregory Palamas, Rublev does not paint the Trinity in its essence (which would be idolatrous), but through its energies, its manifestation in the economy of salvation, "according to the vision of the prophets," according to what has been revealed for our salvation (20). Therefore the Father, whom Rublev depicts on the left, is almost "completely veiled," since we know of him only through the Son and the Spirit, both of whom Irenaeus of Lyons called the Father's "two hands" (96). And both the Son and Spirit bow toward the upright Father. In addition, Bunge draws attention to the fact that although Christ is in the center of the composition and his right hand blesses the Eucharist, the "Father's focus is on the Spirit" (102). Rublev offers a subtle yet powerful articulation of the monarchy of the Father, the distinctive Eastern comprehension of the Trinity, which has resulted in the stiff and aggressive resistance of the Orthodox Church for a millennium to the so-called "double procession" of the Spirit from both "the Father *and the Son*" (Latin "*filioque*"), to quote the Western version of the Nicene Creed. And so Bunge suggests that the icon is a distinctive articulation of the work of the Holy Spirit, who, being sent by the Father (John 15: 26), reveals the Son (1 Cor 12: 3). In addition, given its commission by the Trinity monastery, with its origins in Sergii's devotion to the Holy Spirit in the *mysterium Trinitatis*, the Rublev Trinity offers a powerful and highly original contribution to the aesthetic experience of the Holy Spirit (81).

Bunge suggests that given the orientation of the altar, the viewer is actually experiencing the intimate "wordless" conversation between Father, Son, and Spirit, from behind the altar, that is, in communion with this divine mystery. The praying believer is thus given a vision of the Father eternally begetting the Son, the Spirit eternally proceeding from the Father, and both the Son and Spirit glorifying, and thus revealing, the Father. The icon, then, like the Trinity itself, is not static and disinterested, but dynamic, active, working to enfold *us* in its embrace.

There remains so much more to Bunge's rich meditation on the Rublev Trinity than art history. Not only is the Holy Trinity the result of Rublev's own spiritual formation, but also Bunge's writing is clearly the product of prayer and fasting, through which he, following the Christian theologian Pseudo-Dionysius, "plunges into the truly mysterious darkness of unknowing," of the *mysterium Trinitatis*. And it is not too much of a stretch to suggest that this text should also be read in the same way. For in the last analysis, as Bunge observes in a profound meditation at the end of the book, what is experienced when this icon is contemplated is "My being, my salvation, as the subject of conversation between the Father, Son, and Spirit" (111). So in the contemplation of and participation in this icon, the Trinity becomes more than merely a dogma of the church to which one gives intellectual assent. It is where the gospel itself, and thus my life, my salvation, is found.

Word and Sacrament

The triune relationship is enacted around the altar, at the Lord's Supper. For the conversation between Father, Son, and Holy Spirit, is given in and through the Word—both verbally in proclamation and sacramentally through holy baptism, the Lord's Supper, confession, and absolution. Oswald Bayer writes that the Lord's Supper "highlights the mutuality of the word and the body, where the body functions verbally and the word operates bodily."[30] And a role for aesthetic experience is found in this mutuality, in which the word is heard, seen, and felt, the body is seen, touched, tasted, and heard. The icon is a reminder that God comes to us, as J. G. Hamann says, "through the creature to the creature," that is, through our aesthetic experience of hearing, seeing, touching, and tasting. To isolate the proclamation of the Word, including preaching the Scriptures, from aesthetic experience, as if the words of the Bible are merely descriptions about Jesus rather than Jesus himself, is to do violence to word and image, the Word and sacrament, sermons and icons. The Rublev Trinity is a reminder that this action is Trinitarian at its core. "Every action of the triune God," Bayer states, "is a promise that gives and a gift that promises."[31] What does the Rublev Trinity, that icon of the Holy Spirit, born into and from the deep tradition of Trinitarian spirituality, promise?

Jesus.

It gives what only Alyosha in Dostoyevsky's *The Brother Karamazov* can give his atheistic brother, Ivan, in defense of God in the face of the world's suffering. It gives Jesus, crucified for us. It is important to remember that Nicaea II, the seventh ecumenical council, which dealt with the iconoclastic controversy, did not merely allow for painted depictions of Christ, but it even required them in order to preserve his humanity. Nicaea II, like the preceding councils, always had Christology as its focus. The icon, then, gives Jesus, who promises, "I will never leave you nor forsake you," and gives it to us—*to you and to me*. It is Jesus who discloses the Trinity to us, Jesus who testifies of the Father and is illumined by the Holy Spirit. To look at the Rublev Trinity is to contemplate the "all in all," to be interpreted by that which has drawn, is drawing, and will draw the world to itself (1 Cor 15:28).

Tarkovsky's Rublev

Tarkovsky's masterpiece, *The Passion According to Andrei*, is a reflection on artistic genius that was inspired by the filmmaker's experience of seeing the Rublev Trinity. Tarkovsky explains, "I wanted to use the example of Rublev to explore the question of the psychology of artistic creativity, and analyze the mentality and civic awareness of an artist who created spiritual treasures of timeless significance."[32] And Rublev "expresses the hope and moral ideal of an entire people, and not only the artist's subjective reaction to the world

---

30. Bayer, *Martin Luther's Theology*, 90.

31. Ibid., 91.

32. Tarkovsky, *Sculpting in Time*, 34.

around him."[33] Although Tarkovsky is interested primarily with how the Rublev Trinity rises out of pain and suffering, Bunge's essay reveals how the very subject of the icon, the Holy Trinity, comes down to us—meets us in that pain and suffering. The Rublev Trinity is not a painting of an idea, a concept, dogma, or doctrine. It is an aesthetic experience of hope in the promise that it is through Christ, the one who suffered for us, that "all things" were made and through whom "all things" hold together (Col 1), that I am ultimately known. "To make God known," as Oswald Bayer states, "is the office of Jesus Christ."[34] And in the icon, Christ comes to us in and under the weakness of dirt and wood and through the broken, doubting, and struggling brush of a man, Andrei Rublev. Martin Luther wrote, "God does not deal nor has he ever dealt with us except through the word of promise. We, in turn, cannot deal with God except through faith in the word of his promise."[35] The Rublev Trinity operates within this embodied word of promise in paint and wood. And so what it requires and offers is faith.

If faith in the Rublev Trinity makes God certain, perhaps, then, it might even be possible to say: The icon of the Holy Trinity by Andrei Rublev exists, therefore art exists.

ROBYN O'NEIL'S *HELL*

In order to be reborn, one must first die.

—ROBYN O'NEIL

"The aim of art," claimed Russian filmmaker Andrei Tarkovsky, "is to prepare a person for death, to plough and harrow his soul, rendering it capable of turning to good."[36] That such weak, vulnerable, and comparatively insignificant artifacts as images printed on celluloid, pigments smeared on a canvas, or graphite marks scratched on a piece of paper could be involved in such a serious endeavor is beyond our comprehension. But works of art can indeed "plough and harrow" the soul, when they are interwoven with death

---

33. Ibid., 22.

34. Bayer, *Freedom in Response*, 60.

35. Quoted in Bayer, *Martin Luther's Theology*, 89.

36. Tarkovsky, *Sculpting in Time*, 43.

and loss, and are the material means by which we come to learn something of ourselves and the world. And it can happen in unusual ways.

Hurricane Sandy

Like many artists whose work is represented by galleries in the neighborhood of Chelsea in Manhattan, Robyn O'Neil was adversely affected by the flooding caused by Hurricane Sandy in late October 2012. In fact, the flood destroyed the most important work of her career, a drawing seven feet high and fourteen feet long and in three parts, which featured 65,000 figures and 35,000 collage elements that took her over two years of obsessive work to make. It was also a work that nearly killed her.

Who is Robyn O'Neil?

Born in Omaha, Nebraska in 1977, Robyn O'Neil had spent most of her career as an artist working in Houston, Texas before relocating to Los Angeles. Known for large scale, labor-intensive narrative drawings, O'Neil's work has been featured in numerous group exhibitions, such as the 2004 Whitney Biennial and the American Folk Art Museum in New York City and the Museum of Contemporary Art in Chicago, as well as solo museum exhibitions at The Des Moines Art Center and the Contemporary Arts Museum in Houston. Her work is represented by Praz-Delavellade Gallery in Paris and Berlin; Susan Inglett Gallery in New York City; and Talley Dunn Gallery in Dallas, where I first saw and wrote about her work in 2006. An artist of prodigious literary and cinematic interests, O'Neil has, since moving to Los Angeles, turned to film and opera after studying at Werner Herzog's Rogue Film School in Los Angeles.[37]

"The Sweat Suit Guys"

The heart of O'Neil's work for nearly a decade has been an epic and absurd narrative featuring groups of men in sweat suits and Nikes performing various odd and futile actions. It is an apocalyptic project, a project

---

37. For more information about Robyn O'Neil and her work, see her website, http://robynoneil.com; an online interview in *The Believer*, http://www.believer-mag.com/issues/200811/?read=interview_oneil; and this podcast interview, http://notesonlooking.com/2012/08/robyn-oneil-on-surviving-a-hangoverfrom-hell-and-other-harrowing-tales-on-the-conversation-podcast/.

that narrates The End. In contrast to the meticulously and naturalistically drawn landscape and its flora and fauna, these men are drawn awkwardly, a stylistic device deployed by O'Neil that suggests their discomfort in and antagonistic relationship to their environment. About this stylistic disparity, O'Neil observes,

> Humans are not sure of their place here on earth. They're tense and uneasy. Unnatural and too complicated. Animals, however, are aware and know what to do with themselves. They live gracefully and with clear purpose.[38]

The men, whom O'Neil regards as an "archetype for humanity," are absurd creatures who "do terrible things" and because there are no women to propagate the species, no hope for a future, they lack the power to create a tomorrow. Living in constant tension and discomfort with their world, the "sweat suit guys" seem oblivious to their fate. These men reminded me of Pascal's declaration on the dichotomies of humanity:

> What a chimera, then, is man! What a novelty, what a monster, what a chaos, what a subject of contradiction, what a prodigy! A judge of all things, feeble work of the earth . . . the glory and the shame of the universe![39]

Figure 1

O'Neil finally was able to bring her epic yet meandering narrative to an end with *These final hours embrace at last; this is our ending, this is our past*

38. Quoted in online interview, "From the Desk of: Robyn O'Neil," July 12, 2011, http://fromyourdesks.com/2011/07/12/robyn-oneil/.

39. Pascal, *Pensées*, 36.

(2007), a dramatic composition featuring the lone survivor hanging from a line as waves, presumably from a colossal flood, consume the world (figure 1). The drawing conjures Nietzsche's Zarathustra, who proclaims, "Man is a rope stretched between the animal and the Overman—a rope over an abyss."[40] My first encounter with O'Neil's work came at the exhibition of this and other related "last works" in Dallas, in 2006. And I was struck by two things: first, the sheer physical difficulty and challenge of executing these deceptively simply works. Armed with only a .5mm mechanical pencil, O'Neil covers massive sheets of paper with her intricate compositions. Her task of filling paper with graphite marks becomes an intense ascetic practice, one that tests her physical endurance. The second characteristic of the work that impressed me was the still small voice of hope, a faint hope or an expectation of a day after. O'Neil has observed, "I'd say my work has contained this percentage: 75% conflict, 21% death, and 4% hope."[41]

And it was this "4%" of hope that I emphasized in my writing about her work—and emerging as it did from this apocalyptic sense of an "after" The End, I understood her narrative as a religious project, one in the vein of Wittgenstein's famous statement: "I am not a religious man but I cannot help seeing every problem from a religious point of view."[42] My experience of O'Neil's work was shaped as it was by this drawing—a drawing that, despite all evidence to the contrary, seemed to secrete hope.

In a catalogue essay for Robyn O'Neil's exhibition at the Des Moines Art Center in 2010, I wrote:

> With *This is our ending, this is our past.*, a small exhibition of five large drawings exhibited in 2007 at Dunn and Brown Contemporary in Dallas, Texas, she has brought the End to an abrupt end. This is a courageous act. O'Neil refuses to give in to the narcotic of self-indulgent despair and moralizing. Her seven-year project on the End, from which this exhibition at the Des Moines Art Center is based, is a battle to defeat it, to recognize it for what it is, and to overcome it.[43]

What I did not realize was that the End had not come, that O'Neil had not brought the apocalypse to an end, had not defeated it. And certainly had not overcome it.

40. Nietzsche, "Thus Spoke Zarathustra," 126.

41. Quoted in ibid.

42. Quoted in Kerr, *Theology After Wittgenstein*, 33.

43. Siedell, "After the End: The Artistic Practice of Hope," in *The world has won. A final bow was taken.*, 57.

Hell on Earth and the Impossibility of Making Your Own Ending

When she moved her studio from Houston to Los Angeles in late 2010, O'Neil brought with her a colossal drawing that challenged her physical health and mental endurance. While reveling in the joy of finally being rid of the burden of drawing the sweat suit guys, which had shaped her identity as an artist, the guys that garnered her so much art world attention and acclaim, the guys that even earned her a commission from *The New York Times* to make a drawing of them wearing the new Chanel fall line in 2005 — in short, of being rid of the narrative that gave shape to her life as an artist, the idea came to O'Neil to portray the sweat suit guys in an afterlife. It was a drawing—the most ambitious and physically demanding to date—that was supposed to *really* put an end to what had already ended. Although she usually creates the elaborate titles for her works after she has made them, this one was different. She knew the title before she started work on the drawing.

She called it *Hell*. "I had to make them in hell," O'Neil explained in an interview. "I wanted art to kill them . . . *And then I wanted to torture them.*" Moreover, she also observed, "It felt like something I had to do" and that "it had to be a painful experience for me."[44] The work took over two years to complete, two years of obsessive work that dominated her life and damaged her health to an even greater degree than her previous drawings. O'Neil finally finished the work and sent it to New York for an exhibition at Susan Inglett Gallery in New York City. And to her surprise, it received very little critical attention.

Figure 2

44. http://notesonlooking.com/2012/08/robyn-oneil-on-surviving-a-hangover-from-hell-and-other-harrowing-tales-on-the-conversation-podcast/.

O'Neil, *Hell*, and Me

In the summer of 2011 O'Neil invited me to the opening of the exhibition in New York. She told me she was working eighteen hours a day and would continue to do so for the next two months in order to complete it. She said she was in over her head. She said she was exhausted. And she said that of all the people she knew in the world, I would appreciate most what she was doing in that drawing.

But, I wasn't able to make the exhibition.

Not long after her exhibition, Hurricane Sandy hit New York and in the following days O'Neil sent me an email that *Hell* (figure 2) had been destroyed.

Under the very best circumstances, making a work of art is an absurd risk, and by the standards of the world, a waste of time and effort, and so I cannot imagine the void that an artist feels, the black hole that emerges, when a work of art is lost. Yet I cannot deny my own loss. O'Neil's work exists in my imagination as a series of discrete experiences. And my anticipation of seeing this drawing and how it would affect my experience of O'Neil's previous drawings was an important part of my ongoing relationship with her work. Her loss was, in some way, mine as well. I had plans for it—not just to see it but to write about it, perhaps even to exhibit it. But this most important drawing, which cost the artist so much, this drawing that she wanted me to see, survives now for me only in photographs—a gigantic piece of the artistic puzzle of O'Neil's art and life that is forever lost.

In the days and months that followed, I comforted myself with the knowledge that *Hell* would continue to exist for O'Neil, continuing to exert its absent presence on her work and life. As for me, I still held hope for *Hell*, that the drawing that almost killed its maker has a future for me—that even its absence would serve to deepen my understanding of her work.

"From the Depths of the Earth/You Will Again Bring Me Up" (Psalm 72:20)

The loss of *Hell*, however, revealed a darker side to O'Neil's obsessive artistic practice and the narrative project that drove her work for so many years, a darker side that I have only recently become aware of as the artist has spoken about the fate of the drawing. After her most recognizable work, *These final hours embrace at last; this is our ending, this is our past* (2007) was acquired by the Modern Art Museum of Fort Worth, O'Neil gave a public lecture at the museum entitled "Ending Things."[45] The lecture revealed the suffocating pressure that O'Neil experienced working within this narrative, a narrative that she tried desperately to bring to an end. The "sweat suit guys" narrative was more than an obsession, it was destroying O'Neil and she was powerless to escape it. An artist obsessed with The End could not bring her own narrative to an end.

But what O'Neil was powerless to do, Hurricane Sandy did. The damage that the storm caused to *Hell* liberated O'Neil by killing the project once and for all. The completion of *Hell* apparently could not end it. About the loss of *Hell*, O'Neil observed, "it's the best thing that's ever happened to me. My work has changed in ways it needed to." Moreover, O'Neil realized that the narrative had limited her creativity as an artist while also depriving her of the capacity to live creatively and spontaneously as a human being. (In making *Hell*, she even worked while she went to the bathroom.) "I regret the amount of time I spent with no sense of discovery." And now she has been given space to breathe and time to discover, to develop a studio practice that is receptive and responsive to the world in ways she had never previously enjoyed as an artist. And perhaps even more striking is O'Neil's confession that now, after the destruction of *Hell*, "I'm a different human being." The storm that destroyed *Hell* has offered her new life, in part by forcing her to recognize and confront her obsessions. Perhaps it was appropriate that the apocalyptic hurricane wave that destroyed the sweat suit guys, leaving only one man dangling from a wire, also destroyed *Hell* and freed O'Neil. The great and idiosyncratic critic of the Enlightenment, J. G. Hamann, wrote, "Nothing but the descent into the hell of self-knowledge prepares our way to deification."[46] The making—but more importantly and necessarily—the *destruction* of *Hell* offered her this necessary descent. O'Neil admits that although she had wanted to end this obsessive practice for some time, *"I needed something bigger than me."*

The Critic

The art critic who follows closely the work of an artist is always trying to catch up, in pursuit of the artist on the path that he or she is clearing out. And so the critic's discoveries about an artist's work are always tentative, as the artist never stops cutting new paths with each new work. And so the practice of art criticism, especially the practice that aims to follow an artist

45. See O'Neil's lecture at http://themodern.org/programs/past/Robyn-ONeil/1818. All quotations are from the audio lecture.

46. Quoted in Bayer, *A Contemporary in Dissent*, 61.

over time, is the practice of revision, of writing from a position that will always change, often not long after those conclusions go into print. The only hope that the critic has is that the artist can recognize or discover in the critic's sentences something of where he or she has been, or that the critic's work somehow places its finger on a pulse that continues to drive the artist's new discoveries, revealing them for a reader. My work as a critic is motivated by the desire to find that pulse, or that flowing subterranean tributary, that feeds the distinctive artistic identity. And my practice as a critic has shown me that my successes at finding that tributary always seem to lead me to somewhere else, somewhere deeper. There is always something more to say about an artist like Robyn O'Neil and her work because there is always more to find, ever-deeper tributaries that reveal her inexhaustible and complex humanity, of which her artistic artifacts are tantalizing and at times perplexing signposts.

And yet, my work as a critic is concerned ultimately with the effect the work has on me, as the works I interpret interpret me first. That is, quite frankly, why I feel compelled to follow some artists on the paths they create for themselves—I believe that their discoveries will help me to discover something about myself and the world, as well as the God I stand before. O'Neil happens to be one of these artists.

Hope

In her description of her lecture, "Ending Things" at the Modern Art Museum in Fort Worth, O'Neil writes,

> Endings can be inconclusive, but yet are still called "endings." They are also starting points; things must end so that something else will happen. In order to be reborn, one must first die.

What O'Neil's work reveals is that "death" is not just an aesthetic phenomenon, or a creative device, something that an artist uses to get someplace else, leaving his or her self firmly intact, firmly in control. In other words, "death" cannot come from within the narrative; it cannot be brought about by the subject. Indeed, it is something that the artist suffers passively, from the outside, and it must destabilize that self, perhaps even in some way destroy it. And this death cannot be anticipated and the pain softened. It can only be appreciated and understood retrospectively, on the other side of death.

There is hope after all in O'Neil's ten-year project. But it came first by way of despair. There is life after The End. But it comes only by way of death and destruction.

This seems to be the way of art. And one of the ways it can "plough and harrow" one's soul—the artist's and the viewer's.

> "The Lord brings death and makes alive;
> he brings down to the grave and
> raises up (1 Sam 2:6).

LARKS THAT CANNOT SING: AN ARTISTIC MEDITATION ON THE HOLY INNOCENTS

A voice is heard in Ramah,
weeping and great mourning,
Rachel weeping for her children
and refusing to be comforted,
because they are no more.

—JEREMIAH 31:15

We tend to believe that since a work of art hangs on a wall or sits on a pedestal, that it is a static thing, and so requires our interpretation to bring it to life. But in reality, a work of art has its own agency. It speaks, and we respond. And it often does so long after we leave the museum, gallery, or artist's studio. A work of art is like a magnet—attracting, collecting, and accumulating our thoughts and experiences over time. It insinuates itself in our daily experiences, our thoughts, it finds its way into the books we read, the music we listen to, the conversations we have with friends and coworkers. It crawls into our psychological nooks and crannies. We may not be consciously thinking about a work of art, but it is there, just below our experiential surface. It enables, or, as the case can often be, forces us to confront the reality of our lived experience in different and deeper ways.

A Novel and a Sermon

This happened to me in a particularly powerful way while listening to a sermon delivered on the occasion of the martyrdom of the Holy Innocents, which commemorates those children in Bethlehem slaughtered by Herod in an attempt to destroy the Jewish Messiah (Matt 2:13). The heartrending and gratuitous nature of the suffering of children is a serious challenge to the Christian understanding of God as defined by love (1 John 4:8). One of the most poignant examples of this is in Dostoyevsky's *Brothers Karamazov* when the atheist Ivan asks his brother, Alyosha, the Orthodox monk:

> And are you able to allow the idea that the people for whom you are constructing the edifice would themselves agree to accept their happiness being bought by the unwarranted blood of a small, tortured child and, having accepted it, remain happy forever?[47]

I once heard a powerful sermon on this question by my friend, Dr. Jonathan A. Linebaugh, at Coral Ridge Presbyterian Church. At the time I was reading Victor Hugo's epic novel, *Les Misérables*, and thinking a lot about Cosette's suffering as a child. Dr. Linebaugh's sermon asked, "What does Christmas have to say to the slaughter of babies under Herod or to the school shootings at the kindergarten in Newtown, Connecticut?" And with the Holy Innocents and Cosette on my mind, the paintings, watercolors, and clay sculpture of Claudia Alvarez, with which I have a long relationship, joined the conversation.

Claudia Alvarez and Her Children

Born in Monterrey, Mexico, Alvarez moved to the United States when she was three years old. The New York-based artist studied art at the University of Cal-Davis and the California School of Arts, and has served as an artist in residence in Mexico, Switzerland, France, and China. Her work has been exhibited throughout the United States, Europe, and Canada.

Since 2000 Alvarez has made paintings and clay sculptures that depict children in unusual contexts and disturbing situations. Her work has been a continual source of reflection since I first saw a reproduction of *Bruised Sky* (2005) while serving as a juror for a residency program at the Bemis Center for Contemporary Art in Omaha nearly ten years ago. A ceramic sculpture installation, *Bruised Sky* consists of eight children, each of whom are missing all or parts of arms and with chairs, tables, or birds perched on their heads, looking up into the sky in expectation of an arrival or delivery. Alvarez's interest in children as subject matter came out of her experience working with terminally ill children for twelve years as a non-emergency

---

47. Dostoyevsky, *The Brothers Karamazov*, 282.

ambulance driver for the California Davis Medical Center in Sacramento. "In the process of dying," Alvarez explains, "I saw in the children strength, pain, innocence, and hope."[48] She continues,

> I began to explore the potential of children as surrogates to embody psychological and sociological structures of behavior and the human condition. This investigation evolved over time to include exploring complex social themes related to ethics, culture, and belief systems.[49]

Alvarez's drawings, paintings, and clay sculptures consist of children— alone, in pairs, or in groups—carrying guns, smoking cigarettes, or involved in violent acts and with either aggressive or erotic expressions. The rough-hewn painted textures that reveal the tactile sensuality of Alvarez's brush-work suggest very adult and life-worn emotions and experiences. And yet most of her children are also profoundly vulnerable. Whether in painting or sculpture, these children are either not clothed or dressed in pajamas, even sucking on a pacifier or their fingers, as in *Flower Girl*, which depicts a young child in underpants crouching in fear and sucking her fingers.

Alvarez's children are disconcerting—they *look* like children but they don't *feel* like children. They are harsh. It is not hard to imagine that Victor Hugo's description of the young orphan Cosette in *Les Misérables* applies to these creatures: "injustice had made her sullen, and misery had made her ugly."[50]

Alvarez's girls *were* innocent and beautiful. And we see glimpses of it—the pink sleeper and the yellow Binky in *El Chupon*, for example. But they live in an adult world—they smoke, carry guns, and glare. They are also deprived—deprived of limbs (*Falling Rope of Silence*), clothes, joy, and faith. These creatures trust no one because they have not been loved.

In Alvarez's ceramic sculptures, the crouching figures occupy our space, haunting us with their presence. In her paintings, the figures seem to emerge, often only partially, from an ominous atmosphere. But what is it that bothers me about these children? What is so strange about them?

Fear.

They are afraid. They are not afraid of childish things, like the dark, or the bogeyman.

Alvarez's children experience the fear that characterizes adult life, that existential suffering that drains the world of its enchantment and wonder,

48. Conversation with the author.

49. Ibid.

50. Hugo, *Les Misérables*, 157.

its grace and love. We call this fear something else in the adult world—we like to call it "reality," determination, passion, courage, strength—a whole glossary of euphemisms that masks the terror that we live with on a daily basis. Every day is a fight—a fight for justification and recognition. We feel it. And we can barely remember the innocence and wonder we experienced in our childhood. We do not want our children to feel *that* yet, that disillusionment and disenchantment. And so Alvarez's children haven't learned to hide these adult concerns, hide their experience of the "real world" (as opposed to the fantasy world of childhood that we "outgrow" and mature beyond). And so it deforms them, transforms them into something other than children.

And this is what Alvarez's children have become—something other than children. Again, I think of Hugo's Cosette. The villagers give her a nickname. They call her the lark. Hugo tells us why:

> No larger than a bird, trembling, frightened, and shivering, first to wake every morning in the house and the village, always in the street or in the fields before dawn.[51]

But Hugo continues, "except that the poor lark never sang." Cosette lurks behind the eyes of *The Flower Girl* and most of the children Alvarez paints or models from clay.

A child is made to sing. And there is something evil about a child who cannot sing, a child who cannot play. Alvarez's children are silent and they do not play.

Childhood Enchantments, Wounds, and Christmas

Children elicit our strongest emotions, our most passionate responses to and desires for this world. They embody our hope that the world really is, deep down, good. It is the world of Christmas morning. But Alvarez's work offers us something else, what C. S. Lewis wrote about Narnia under the rule of the White Witch—it is always winter but never Christmas. This is what we want to protect our children from—from *our fear* that there really isn't Christmas, or that the enchantments we experienced as children will never be relived. But Alvarez's work refuses to play along.

Alvarez's work is powerful in large part because it yanks the idea of childhood from the fog of idealization *and* idolization. Childhood is not merely the time of innocent enchantments but also of deep wounds, wounds which abide into adulthood and shape the development of who we are and

51. Ibid.

shall be. Perhaps our idealization of childhood is a refusal to acknowledge those childhood wounds that we all bear.

Her work reminds us that children are not born into Disneyland. They are often born into Ethiopia, into ER incubators, into crack houses—into murder, starvation, and suffering. They are also born into comfortable and stable two-parent homes in the suburbs full of love that nevertheless cannot prevent them from experiencing deep wounds. Alvarez's work forces me to ask, where is God in the suffering of a child? The suffering does not have to be the murder under Herod or abuse at the hands of a pedophile, but the kind of quiet suffering every child experiences—that my children have experienced. How can God create such beautiful larks that cannot sing, larks that bear such dreadful wounds? Perhaps at the end of the day Alvarez's work is powerful because it touches our own childhood wounds, reminds us that our childhood experience was one that included pain and suffering.

So, what does Christmas have to do with Claudia Alvarez's children? The only answer is the one that Dr. Linebaugh offered one Sunday at Coral Ridge, the same answer that Alyosha gives his older brother, Ivan. And the same answer we offer to those babies killed in Bethlehem under Herod.

Jesus.

The child who was born to suffer and die for us. The one who asks us to come to him as children (Matt 18:3–4). The one who kisses us ("Let him kiss me with the kisses of his mouth"—Song 1:1). Even Alyosha's brother, Ivan, who offers his "poem" of the Grand Inquisitor, has Jesus respond to the Inquisitor's demand to give an account for humanity's suffering by simply kissing him on the forehead.[52]

And this the one who makes us all children through faith, giving us a song to sing, perhaps a kiss, even in the suffering.

---

52. Dostoyevsky, *The Brothers Karamazov*, 302.

6

THE POETICS
OF MODERN ART

For Modernism is but a logical consequence—compression and concision—of things classical.

—JOSEPH BRODSKY

No one absorbs the past as thoroughly as a poet, if only out of fear of inventing the already invented.

—JOSEPH BRODSKY

To create living art—this is my goal.

—GUSTAVE COURBET

MODERN ART AND TRADITION

Modern art is often celebrated as well as vilified for liberating art from the shackles of the past and the burdens of tradition. Yet this is not an accurate description of the modern artist's relationship to the past. Despite their desire to free themselves from what they experienced as the suffocating confines of tradition, modern artists were deeply interested in the art of the past, in discovering or reviving alternative traditions, if only as a means to be more faithful to their own personalities and sensibilities. Moreover, modern art itself has become a robust and dynamic living tradition, which shapes artistic practice in the present.

Writing in 1848, Gustave Courbet explained, "I simply wanted to draw forth from a complete acquaintance with tradition the reasoned and independent consciousness of my own individuality" in order "to be in a position to translate the customs, the ideas, and appearance of my epoch, according to my own estimation . . ."[1] The artist's relationship to the art of the past is one of the most important, yet often overlooked aspects of the modern artistic tradition.

The Fogg Art Museum, Harvard University, 1970

While Michael Fried was giving colleague and fellow critic Rosalind Krauss a tour of an exhibition of Frank Stella's paintings at the Fogg Art Museum at Harvard University in 1970, a student approached Fried and demanded to know what was so good about the exhibition, which consisted of canvases on which Stella had painted stripes, lines, and chevrons. Krauss recounted Fried's response. "Look," he said slowly, "there are days when Stella goes to the Metropolitan Museum." Fried continued:

> "And he sits for hours looking at the Velázquezes, utterly knocked out by them and then he goes back to his studio. What he would like more than anything else is to paint like Velázquez. But what he knows is that that is an option that is not open to him. So he paints stripes." Fried's voice had risen, "he wants to be Velázquez so *he paints stripes*."[2]

How does looking at Velázquez lead to stripes?
Tradition.

1. Courbet, "Art Cannot Be Taught," 33–34.
2. Krauss, "A View of Modernism," 48.

Tradition and Community

With its optimism, celebration of the new, and amnesia, modernity has taught us to be skeptical of tradition, wary of its ossifying leaven that spoils our individuality and autonomy. It suffocates our freedom, removes us from the realities of contemporary life and throws us into a sepulchre, haranguing us with cranky demands to do things "the way they have always been done." And so we believe that modern art is the apotheosis of this individuality and freedom—liberation from tradition in its perpetual search for the new.

But the history of modern art tells a very different story, one that reveals the important and necessary role of tradition in its development—not merely as something against which to react, but as a space that makes action possible. Literary critic Harold Bloom puts it well when he asks, "What happens if one tries to write, or to teach, or to think, or even to read without the sense of tradition?" He responds, "Why, nothing at all happens, just nothing."[3] Painting is no different. It is a practice that requires practice. It requires imitation, training, and rebellion. It requires a tradition into which the painter is initiated. In Chaim Potok's novel *My Name is Asher Lev*, the master Jacob Kahn warns the young Asher about the training he will undergo:

> Do you understand what this is? . . . This is not a toy. This is not a child scrawling on a wall. This is a tradition; it is a religion, Asher Lev. You are entering a religion called painting. It has its fanatics and its rebels. And I will force you to master it. Do you hear me? No one will listen to what you have to say unless they are convinced you have mastered it. Only one who has mastered a tradition has a right to attempt to add to it or to rebel against it. Do you understand me, Asher Lev?[4]

The education of an artist, then, is an initiation into a tradition. To celebrate or to dismiss radical artists like Picasso and Pollock, Warhol and Hirst because they have disregarded artistic tradition is to misunderstand the communal nature of their work and its role as a creative response. As T. S. Eliot observes in his essay "Tradition and the Individual Talent" (1917),

> No poet, no artist of any art, has his complete meaning alone. His significance, his appreciation is the appreciation of his relation to the dead poets and artists. You cannot value him alone;

---

3. Bloom, *A Map of Misreading*, 32.
4. Potok, *My Name is Asher Lev*, 197.

you must set him, for contrast and comparison, among the dead.[5]

To contrast and compare the artist among the dead is one of the tasks of art criticism, and it is precisely what Michael Fried is doing with Frank Stella in contrasting and comparing him to Velázquez. Criticism reveals what Jaroslav Pelikan called tradition: "the living faith of the dead."[6]

When an artist drags her brush across a canvas for the first time she is merely following what countless artists have done before her and what countless artists will do after her. The education of an artist, therefore, consists of more than the acquisition of technical skills, such as learning to draw, use paint, handle an etching tool, or model a form from clay. It includes learning to behave like an artist. It is the acquisition of a *habitus*, a way of life, a general disposition toward the world *as an artist*, not simply as an autonomous individual but as a part of a community that forms, shapes, and sustains. Picasso somewhere said, "It is not what the artist does that counts. It is what he is."[7] It is indeed true that artistic practice emphasizes and privileges the singular individuality of the artist, even when these artists are participating in a collective avant-garde movement, like Cubism, Surrealism, or Abstract Expressionism. While she often appears solitary in relation to her contemporaries, the modern artist carries with her a great cloud of witnesses, a community, or conversation partners amongst the dead. Therefore, when an artist goes into her studio, she is never alone, and when she drags her brush across that canvas, it is in *response* to the voices that she hears, the conversations that she is having with artists from the past. As Krauss points out, "Stella's need to say something through his art was the same as a 17th-century Spaniard's; only the point in time was different."[8]

Therefore, because they emerge from a conversation and participate in a tradition, paintings need to be understood within that conversation, understood as *responses*. "Our freedom," observes Oswald Bayer, "is a communal interplay between what is given beforehand and what is acquired, what is received and what is passed on."[9] Therefore, knowledge of the history of art—of the artistic conversations that have taken place through the generations—is not only a necessary part of making a painting, it is also a necessary part of looking at paintings. Just as it takes practice to make a painting, it takes practice to look at one as well, practice to understand how

5. Eliot, "Tradition and the Individual Talent" (1917), in *Selected Essays*, 4.

6. Pelikan, *The Vindication of Tradition*.

7. Quoted in Danchev, ed., *The Letters of Paul Cézanne*, 39.

8. Krauss, "A View of Modernism," 48.

9. Bayer, *Freedom in Response*, 251.

Stella, who paints stripes, and Velazquez, who paints portraits, might be trying to say the same thing.

How does a viewer develop this knowledge? She does so the same way an artist does—by losing her claims to autonomy and individuality. She visits art museums and galleries; talks to artists and observes their behaviors and practices; reads biographies of artists whom she admires; reads the work of critics and art historians—in short, she becomes a listener.

Perhaps the most important roles that I played as an art historian working with studio art students was to show them that in order to develop a distinctive artistic voice, they must release their death grip on their nineteen-year-old egos. In fact, their belief that their studio work must come out of this particular self will doom their work to conformity, to what every nineteen-year-old claims to be their authentic self. Furthermore, the development of this authentic self, which will ultimately produce a distinctive artistic vision, will only occur over years and decades, not weeks or months. The educational arc of an artist is thus not limited to the semesters in a degree program, but contains the scope an entire life lived in and for art, *in and through the tradition of living as an artist*. And it is ongoing. Individuality emerges only gradually, on the back end, so to speak—as a *result of* this conversation with the past rather than as its prerequisite.

Tradition and Conflict

The relationship of the modern artist to the past begins, ironically, with the experience of rupture and loss, with an intuition of the deep *discontinuity* between the past and the present, the recognition that artistic depictions of angels and cherubs, nymphs, maidens, and martyrs, which were appropriate responses to a past age. But what is now required are new artistic forms that come from the experience of the present. This approach contradicted the nineteenth-century academic establishment, which saw the art of the past as an ideal that normed all art and that demanded emulation of technique and subject matter that simply needed to be passed on to another generation. For the modern artist, however, art was, and is, not merely the transmission of technique and subject matter, form and content—it also consists of the artist's own sensibility, which necessarily includes an attunement to the age in which one lives.

The important role of the art of the past for the modern artist emerges as a response to this experience of loss, of being cut off from a shared artistic tradition as it was preserved and transmitted by the academic establishment. This loss, this catastrophic scene, has been commonly referred to as "freedom." Yet, as Sartre observed, this is a freedom to which we are condemned, which obligates us, presses in on us. Within the modern artistic tradition, the artist is free to make *anything*. However, the challenge is that she must make *something*. And deprived of the resources of the academic establishment, the modern artist initiates a search for his own—to find his own colleagues, invent his own conversations, his own friends and allies, and his own opponents—in short, to invent his own living tradition from the art of the past. This at times consists of the revival of artists often ignored or marginalized by the academic establishment (e.g., Velázquez, Giotto, Piero della Francesca) or artistic traditions (e.g., Byzantine icons and medieval German sculpture). But most often it consists of reading the great art of the past differently, with different criteria, different eyes. To return to Krauss's observation about the similarities between Stella and Velázquez, that they both want to say the same thing: their dramatically different historical locations demand that they must say it dramatically differently—to say the same thing in the say way as Velázquez is, Krauss implies, a betrayal of the tradition as living and active and responsive to the cultural, social, and political present.

What are they trying to say? One way to respond is that they are both offering *presence*—the concentration, crystallization of an aesthetic experience, of feeling through form that compels the viewer to be responsive to the moment, to the space that is opened up between her and the painting. It is the experience of feeling on the part of the artist what Cézanne called "sensations," whether it is in painting a portrait or painting stripes, which anchors and then unlocks the viewers' experience of feeling at that moment.

And because this catastrophic "freedom" was experienced as a break from the academic establishment, of the institutional matrix that sustained artistic practice, modern artists were left to fend for themselves, to develop this tradition, to reorient themselves to the art of the past on their own and in their own ways. As Harold Bloom writes about the role of the modern critic: "All that a critic, as critic, can give poets is the deadly encouragement that never ceases to remind them of how heavy their inheritance is."[10] The heaviness of this inheritance is often experienced by the modern artist not only as a conversation, but as an argument; not only as a community, but as a challenge, even a fight. Bloom continues, "A poet, I argue in consequence, is not so much a man speaking to men as a man rebelling against being spoken to by a dead man (the precursor) outrageously more alive than himself."[11]

10. Bloom, *A Map of Misreading*, 10.
11. Ibid., 19.

The modern artist, like Stella, finds himself in the unique position of creating his own tradition, a tradition that will in turn exert pressure on him, challenge him—seduce and haunt him. This is why Eliot could write, "there is no freedom in art."[12] The only freedom, what Eliot calls "truly freedom," take place only "against the background of an artificial limitation."[13]

According to Fried, Stella's stripe paintings are a commentary on Velázquez's portraits, a "misreading," even, as Harold Bloom might say—a creative misreading that in bringing out something overlooked in the Spanish master's portraits, that gives Stella creative space. To overlook the important role that the art of the past and tradition play not just in Stella's paintings but in modern art generally, risks distorting its history and overlooking its most profound insights into human experience.

The *Via Passiva* and the Modern Artist

Fried understands Stella's "freedom" to paint anything, even stripes, not as an individual, defiantly autonomous expression that disregards the past, but as a loving and respectful response to the work of an old master, who, in Bloom's words, is "outrageously more alive than himself." This flies in the face of popular approaches to modern art, which celebrate (or condemn) the artist for his liberation from the conventions of the past. Although it is true that they sought to find forms and subjects more appropriate to "modern life," forms and subjects not limited to classical mythology and Judeo-Christian narratives, modern artists were perhaps more obsessed with the art of the past, with the importance of tradition, than their academic and more conservative peers. For the latter, tradition by the mid-nineteenth century had become merely the application of technique, while for the former it was living and active, not constrained by technique.

Far from celebrating their freedom, modern artists experience it as a loss—a condemnation, catastrophe—and understand the impossibility of painting in a vacuum. The history of modern art, within which Stella understands his work to participate, offers space for artists to find new ways to connect to the art of the past, to draw inspiration, to be sure, but also establish lineage. The modern artist is a child charged with the task of inventing his family tree, creating his heritage, from and within which he gladly subjects himself.

The history of modern art, as artists, critics, and historians have written it, has often overlooked the implicit critique of the Enlightenment's fear

12. Eliot, *To Criticize the Critic*, 184.

13. Ibid., 187.

of tradition and received wisdom as well as supreme confidence in the autonomous self. To overlook Stella's relationship to the past, the paintings in
the Metropolitan Museum, to the Velazquez room he visits regularly, is to
overlook the passivity and receptivity of the tradition of modern art. It overlooks the truth that, following theologian Oswald Bayer, "human freedom is
a response, not an echo."[14] For the modern artist, the past is the source, not
the enemy, of freedom.

Fried's Stella is first and foremost a listener. He hears what Velázquez's
paintings have to say to him. Both its supporters and enemies often lose
sight of the fact that the studio is where the artist exercises his freedom as
a response to the world of experience, to the history of other painters. In
many ways, the modern artist is the paradigmatic example of Luther's *via
passiva*, a "passive" life lived perpetually in faithful response to the gracious
gifts given by God, where identity is first and foremost not from action (*via
activa*) or contemplation (*via contempliva*) but from faith. Fried's approach
to Stella suggests that modern art is a particular approach to the world.
Critic Donald B. Kuspit reiterates this when he observes, "Being an artist is
about being a certain kind of subject, not just about making certain kinds
of objects."[15]

What kind of subject is the modern artist? Following the lead of Fried's
Stella, who more than anything wants to paint like Velázquez, who tries to
paint like Velázquez by painting stripes, not portraits, the modern artist is a
self that lives out of and from faith—not only faith that paint smeared across
some canvases by a seventeenth-century Spanish court painter can speak
to an artist in New York in the mid-twentieth century, but that this man's
response to what he hears is to devote his life, to see his life and the world,
to his own paint strokes smeared across scraps of canvas. That which was
possible three centuries ago is still possible today.

Now that is faith.

14. Bayer, *Freedom in Response*, 54.
15. Kuspit, "Forum," 10.

MY KID CAN DO THAT

Unless you turn and become like children, you will never enter the kingdom of Heaven.

—MATTHEW 18:3

I was so much older then; I'm younger than that now.

—BOB DYLAN, "MY BACK PAGES"

We [The White Stripes] were trying to be childish on purpose.

—JACK WHITE

"My kid can do that" is a common accusation leveled against modern artists whose paintings look nothing like the *Mona Lisa*, the Sistine Chapel ceiling, or a Thomas Kinkade print. As a museum curator, I heard this all the time. Modern art frustrates our expectations of what art should look like, how it should behave. We want artists to impress us with their powerful talent to render likeness, entertain us with images that "look real" (i.e., look like a photograph). But we should not to be trusted. We often simply want to be flattered and distracted at the art museum. And so when we happen upon a painting of colors and lines, or a composition of simple lines and distorted shapes, a painting that doesn't amaze us immediately with the artist's technical proficiency, we become offended, dismiss it as the work of a charlatan and condemn it as childish, not worthy of being called art. And so, often, curators and critics who have devoted their lives to studying art usually respond to such accusations by (rightly) demonstrating the remarkable technical skill of the artist or (rightly) stressing certain philosophical and theoretical frameworks necessary to understand the significance of those seemingly fraudulent gestures.

However, my response to those who claim, "my kid can do that" has been different. I respond, "Well, that was the point."

Religion and Modern Art

Modern art emerged in the mid-nineteenth century as a critique of the complex and at times convoluted aesthetic technology of the French academic establishment, a technology that celebrated the master's capacity to offer ever-more complex flourishes on classical or biblical themes, although he was unable and unwilling to connect with the tumultuous changes in modern life—industrialization, urbanization, the emergence of a middle class, and loss of the church's authority in public and private life.

For the modern artist the academy and its aesthetic sophistication had strangled the life out of art. The paintings of courageous heroes and erotic goddesses, prophets and martyrs, reduced the artist's role to reproducing exquisitely rendered figures from classical and biblical texts for the purpose of instruction in virtue on the one hand and diversion on the other. The modern artist also came to understand academic conventions with these paintings of nymphs, cherubs, gods, and goddesses as an escape from, rather than as an engagement with and an exploration of, the mysteries of life. And in fact, modern artists believed that the academic establishment had instrumentalized art, making it serve the didacticism and scientific positivism of the age. Academic masters like Alexandre Cabanel (1823–1889), William-Adolphe Bouguereau (1825–1905), and Jean-Léon Gérôme (1824–1904) could render the likeness of the world (or at least depict the worlds of classical and biblical literature), but could they really "see" the world, "feel" it, "hear" it as mysterious and enchanted, something more than appearances, something that produced a feeling, a "sensation"?

It was in creative response to this awe-inspiring mystery of nature that gave birth to the belief that art could function like religion. Henri de Saint-Simon wrote in 1824 that the artist and poet would make up the new priest class.[16] And so since its emergence in the mid-nineteenth century, modern art often—much to its chagrin and surprise—finds itself talking and walking like religion, offering an aesthetic and poetic alternative to the emergent religion of positivistic science that refused to consider what could not be demonstrated empirically and relished the demystification and disenchantment of the world in order to advance human progress. It is also deeply imbedded spirituality and attraction to religion and repulsion of the artistic sophistry of the academic establishment that led modern art to an unexpected source: childhood.

And this is why modern art also often talks and walks like a child.

---

16. Egbert, "The Idea of 'Avant-Garde' in Art and Politics," 339.

"And a Little Child Shall Lead Them"

At least since Rousseau published *Emile, or On Education* (1762), artists and poets have been fascinated by childhood and the significance of childhood experience—that the transition from child to adult constitutes, in some essential way, a loss. In fact, the history of modernism in its art and literature can be regarded as placing childhood experience—e.g., fairy tales and children's stories—at the heart of culture. About Lewis Carroll's remarkable *Alice* stories, W. H. Auden writes, "there are no good books which are only for children."[17] Indeed, in her celebration of Lewis Carroll, Virginia Woolf claimed "they [the *Alice* stories] are the only books in which we become children."[18]

For the modern artist to become a child was to re-enter the stage of life in which daily life was filled with wonder and enchantment, in which painting, poetry, and song were the natural responses to the world. And it required, in a profound sense, unlearning the way that the academy had taught the artist to represent the world. Picasso once somewhere observed, "It took me four years to paint like Raphael, but a lifetime to paint like a child."

Why were so many modern artists, including and perhaps especially Picasso, attracted to children's drawings? One reason is that a child's capacity to represent the world is not capable of interpreting their experience of the world, which overwhelms them with wonder and awe. We are drawn to their honest and unself-conscious struggle to render the complexity of the world and their experience of it through their inferior skills. It is this gap between their technical competency and the vastness of their subject that attracts us to these drawings. They are great because they *cannot* represent the world. And yet, each line is a sincere one, each figure a vital attempt to capture something that they not only see but hear and feel as well. Their beauty is in their failure.

Paul Gauguin, Paul Klee, and Picasso, among so many others, were attracted to children's drawings precisely because of this gap, this failure, between the wonder of the world and the paucity of skills with which to render it. The modern artist was deeply critical of the academic master's technical complacency—that he actually possessed the skills to render (and thus control) the world through his brush.

17. Auden, "Today's wonder-world needs Alice" (1962), in *Forewords and Afterwords*, 291.

18. Woolf, "Lewis Carroll," 254.

Humility, Faith, and the Modern Artist

Modern art is often condemned for its arrogance—for aching to break free of the shackles of the wisdom of the artistic and moral past, or for making a painting do more than it should, and in its constant haranguing against the establishment and the bourgeoisie.

And yet, in his fascination with childish things, with the drawings of children and with children's stories and fairy tales, the modern artist was painfully aware of human weakness and frailty, the ultimate inadequacy of art compared to the wonders of nature and the world, and the loss of enchantment with the world as a remarkable and wondrous thing, filled with mystery, ultimately incomprehensible. And the only suitable response would be an offering of praise—whether a song, a poem, or a painting.

Or a prayer.

In his rejection of the academic establishment's exaggerated confidence in artistic technologies to capture (and use) nature for its own purposes (entertainment or instruction), the modern artist inadvertently maintained a space for religious faith—especially the Christian gospel of grace—to breathe. Despite its presence as artistic subject matter, the stories of the Bible had been reduced to moralizing myths of heroism and virtue. The church and institutional Christianity was a means of dispensing law, not grace, of maintaining order and conformity, not mercy and forgiveness and the encouragement of joy and wonder and thanksgiving.

It is not insignificant that it is children that Jesus points to and tells us we must become like (Matt 18:3)—that it is the adult that must emulate the child in matters of faith, not the other way around.

Ironically, Christian critics have long condemned modern art for rejecting the form and content of academic painting, seeing in this rejection the modern artist's rejection of "Christian values," presuming, of course, that such values consist first and foremost of law, not grace—discipline and efficiency, not mercy and forgiveness, joy and playfulness.

Joy and Pain

The modern artist often subsumed his virtuosity for the sake of assuming a childlike posture in the face of a terrible and beautiful world, in which forces act upon us despite our attempts to control and manipulate them for our own benefit. Modern art is a lament in paint, an affirmation that we are broken and the world is not as it ought to be. And yet, it offers a childlike faith—perhaps naïve and idealistic—that it is nevertheless worthy of celebration, of praise. And how childlike the response, in the face of such an awesome and overwhelming world, to offer a drawing?

How could Picasso have depicted the atrocities of the bombing of Guernica in 1937 during the horrific Spanish Civil War through anything other than a childlike posture of helpless wonder and incomprehension? *Guernica* is a massive mural, a twenty-five–foot-long witness to art's *inability* to explain or make sense of the world, a child's lament at the unspeakable cruelty that threatens to suffocate the beauty in the world. *Guernica* is Picasso's acceptance of and resistance to the world as it is, the hope that "once upon a time" can and will be, one day, "this time, now."[19]

Modern art reminds us that contrary to our artistic, scientific, and political pretenses to control, we remain helpless children in the face of a world we cannot comprehend, filling us with awe and terror, joy and pain. And the only thing left that we as helpless children can do is to cry out for help and believe that our cry will be answered.

Even my kid can do that.

DARWIN, LANDSCAPE PAINTING, AND JESUS[20]

As a regular visitor to *Arts & Letters Daily*, the broadsheet-style web portal of ideas founded by the late philosopher Denis Dutton and now operated by the *Chronicle of Higher Education*, I was confronted daily with an advertisement for Dutton's book, *The Art Instinct: Beauty, Pleasure, and Human Evolution*. Yet I avoided it. I had grown weary of the creation-evolution and deism-atheism debates that pockmark the Christian media. As a Christian in the arts, a role that comes with many professional disadvantages, I can at least be thankful that my work does not put me in the cross hairs of the science wars. Moreover, from what I had heard and read from biologist Stephen Jay Gould and psychologist Steven Pinker, evolution did not appear to take art too seriously. Gould says that art is a "spandrel," that is, an open space created by necessary architectural structures in the brain, which is "filled in" by art and other kinds of less necessary activities.[21] And Pinker argues that art amounts to "Sunday afternoon projects" and "cheesecake" for the mind.[22] I have heard more-or-less similar views voiced outside the

---

19. Buechner, *Telling the Truth*, 91.

20. A version of this essay was originally published online at *Books & Culture* (2010), www.booksandculture.com/articles/webexclusives/2010/august/darwinlandscape.html.

21. Gould, "Evolution."

22. Pinker, *How the Mind Works*, 524–25.

evolutionary framework by university administrators and college deans, art collectors and curators, and many Christians. *The Art Instinct* seemed yet another argument for undermining the seriousness of art—and hence undermining my own work as a critic, curator, and educator.

However, while scouring the stacks in my university's library, I came across a copy of *The Art Instinct* and decided to read it. To my surprise, Dutton's book has been helpful for thinking about my work as a critic and curator. I leave engagement with the full scope of Dutton's book, including its weaknesses and blind spots, to others.

Dutton reprimands his fellow secular aestheticians and evolutionary scientists for misconstruing the nature of art and devaluing its importance, arguing that they have made too much of cultural differences. Drawing on his own anthropological fieldwork in New Guinea, Dutton argues that artistic practice is cross-cultural and is the product of an evolutionary imprint developed during the nearly two million years of the Pleistocene era, in which *homo sapiens* emerged with its modern-day attributes. Dutton enlists evolutionary biology to demonstrate the universal characteristics of humanity, which art reveals. Even though art is a profoundly historical and contextual practice, it is not so "all the way down": art works and reworks the stuff that has become our genetic imprint. Therefore, it is intellectually lazy for academics to assume that "art" is only a Western concept. Dutton is thus critical of those theorists, like Arthur Danto and George Dickie, who take liminal and boundary-pushing works of art, like Marcel Duchamp's infamous ready-made, *Fountain* (1917) or Andy Warhol's *Brillo Box* (1964), and make them the centerpiece of a theory of art.[23] Rather, Dutton argues, let those "marginal" works remain at the margins, where they were meant to be, and address the cluster of attributes that seem to form the core not only of a Western understanding of art, but perhaps of a cross-cultural one as well.

Dutton also takes on Gould and Pinker. Through his analysis of art and natural selection, Dutton suggests that it is fruitless to argue whether the arts are an adaptation or can be dismissed as by-products of adaptation (like Pinker's cheesecake). Rather, it is more pertinent to "show how their existence and character are connected to Pleistocene interests, preferences, and capacities."[24] Unlike Gould and Pinker, who consider art to be the result of an overdeveloped brain looking to blow off intellectual steam, Dutton argues that art reworks and reactivates fundamental aspects of human consciousness. If Darwin revealed the reality of Tennyson's "Nature, red in tooth

23. See Danto, "The Artworld," and Dickie, *Art and the Aesthetic.*

24. Dutton, *The Art Instinct,* 96.

and claw," Dutton suggests that art is a necessary weapon in this bloody act of survival, for it "provides us with templates, mental maps for emotional life" as we "work out levels of intentionality."[25] For Dutton, art is not primarily about self-expression, celebrating creativity, or even about representing the spiritual or the transcendent. Moreover, art is also not predicated on the presence of "leisure."[26] It involves making decisions in the world.

The most provocative and useful chapter in *The Art Instinct* for me was the first, entitled "Landscape and Longing." Dutton discusses the research project in the mid-1990s of two conceptual artists, Komar and Melamid, called People's Choice Project, which explored which elements of painting people are most likely to prefer. And to their surprise, most responded to a landscape with trees and open areas, water, human figures, and animals. Dutton quotes one of the surprised artists:

> So I'm wondering, maybe the blue landscape is genetically imprinted in us, that it's the paradise within, that we came from the blue landscape and we want it. . . . We now completed polls in many countries—China, Kenya, Iceland, and so on—and the results are strikingly similar. Can you believe it? Kenya and Iceland—what can be more different in the whole fucking world—and both want blue landscapes.[27]

No matter where the respondents lived and the landscapes with which they were most familiar, no matter their cultural or social upbringing, the majority responded in the same way. For Dutton this is not, as Arthur Danto argued in his review of the project in *The Nation*, because people around the world have been hopelessly influenced by calendar art, but because it is part of our genetic template developed in the African savannas during the end of the Pleistocene era 50,000 years ago. Dutton concludes, "human landscape tastes are not just products of social conditioning"; rather, they reflect "prehistoric tastes."[28]

I did not expect this.

The landscape that confronted our ancient ancestors, Dutton argues, was a landscape that required decision-making: follow the river where threatening animals might be, or take another course? Our survival depended on the wise decisions of our prehistoric relatives. Dutton suggests that the pleasure we experience with some painting is due to its capacity to touch or rekindle this genetic template, stirring up within us these life-and-death

25. Ibid., 111.
26. See for example Scruton, *Culture Counts*, 16–27.
27. Quoted in Dutton, *The Art Instinct*, 15.
28. Ibid, 3.

decisions, making them present to us. As is the case with fiction, landscape painting makes use of two important elements, a human will and some kind of resistance to it. "We are what we are today," Dutton writes, "because our primordial ancestors followed paths/riverbeds over the horizon. At such moments we confront remnants of our own species' ancient past."[29] Art has the potential—and perhaps the responsibility—to bring such remnants into the present, our present.

The implications of this argument are significant. The power of this genetic landscape template is the source of both kitsch and authentic art, popular imagery and high art, the source of Thomas Kinkade and Bob Ross as well as Vincent van Gogh and Edvard Munch. While the former skim off the top of this genetic imprint, the latter plumb its emotional depths, rework it, and present it anew. Perhaps one of the roles of art criticism is to show how and in what ways the work of art participates in enlivening this genetic imprint.

The Wanderer

Dutton's book sheds light on a curatorial project I organized in the fall of 2010, entitled *The Wanderer: Foreign Landscapes of Enrique Martínez Celaya*, at the Museum of Biblical Art (MoBIA) in New York City.[30] The exhibition explored the theme of figure and landscape in Martínez Celaya's work through the lens of the biblical narratives that have influenced his work indirectly through his reading of Robert Frost, Herman Melville, Leo Tolstoy, Søren Kierkegaard, and Herman Hesse, among many others. The biblical narratives are much more than illustrations of themes like exile, exodus, atonement, salvation, sacrifice, redemption, and forgiveness. They are concrete and particular instances of the figure in the landscape, whether Adam, Cain, Abraham, Moses, Jonah, Jesus, or Paul, who are called, at a particular moment, to act in the world. Whether patriarch, prophet, king, disciple, leper, or beggar, the person who acts, in obedience or in defiance of God, must choose to act and must do so alone. Yet we cannot contemplate this structural framework of figure and landscape at a distance. We must choose with the person who is called to act. Jesus, who recapitulates and embodies the entire figure and landscape tradition in the biblical narratives, demands an answer—

29. Ibid., 28.

30. See Siedell, "The Mark of Cain." The essay explores the MoBIA exhibition as well as the simultaneous installation, called *The Crossing*, at the Cathedral Church of Saint John the Divine, New York City.

But who do you say that I am? (Mark 8:29)

Dutton's book suggests that the power of art lies somewhere near this demand to choose, to act in the world with conviction. Perhaps the power of the biblical narratives—including those of the writers influenced by them, as well as Martínez Celaya's work, which is an aesthetic reflection on these narratives—is due *in part* to their capacity to participate in and creatively rework the genetic imprint of the Pleistocene landscape, a genetic imprint that bears witness to our experience of the world as exiles and wanderers, facing danger all around us. And yet art might promise something else, that despite this danger and fear, the landscape might also be a gift—more than simply a stage for our wanderings, but a home.

THE WONDERFUL CONTRADICTIONS OF ABSTRACT PAINTING

It is surely no coincidence that the most memorable experiences I have had with art have occurred when I was with an artist. For although they know that a painting is much more than meets the eye, artists know that this can only be experienced when someone really opens their eyes and looks, looks with their heart and with their ears.

New York City, 1990

My approach to abstract painting changed nearly twenty-five years ago during a conversation with an artist friend in front of Kasimir Malevich's *White on White* (1918) at a retrospective exhibition of the artist's work at the Metropolitan Museum of Art.

As we stood in front of the painting, I was telling my friend about Malevich's theories of abstraction and his utopian belief that paintings of squares and rectangles could transform society. My friend interrupted me and, with his nose about as close as one could get to the painting, whispered, "Look at this surface! How did he do it?" As I looked at that meticulously worked-over canvas, *White on White* became something other than a visual illustration of an idea, or a theory, or a historical artifact. It became a painting—a vulnerable, futile, and weak object, lovingly and painstakingly made by a human being in the midst of a world turned upside-down by World War I and the Russian Revolution.

All of a sudden, Malevich's rhetoric about the "supremacy of pure feeling or perception in the pictorial arts" and his desire to "free art from the ballast of the objective world" faded away, as did all my art history and art theory, and I was brought face-to-face with a surprising fact. In the midst of chaos and exhilaration, of hope for a new world and a new humanity, Malevich painted a picture of a white rectangle on a white background. What a wonderfully absurd thing to do. And what an odd—and defiant—response to the Russian Revolution. But perhaps more surprising, I experienced its defiance directed at me, the art history graduate student, the theoretician, the one with a head full of ideas. *White on White* seemed to cut through all of that noise to confront me not as a would-be professor and scholar, but as a human being who was busy with thoughts about how his work was going to transform fields of study. It offered new ways of thinking about modern art.

New York City, 2013

I thought about my initial encounter with Malevich's *White on White* after running into it again as I walked through the galleries of *Inventing Abstraction: 1910–1925*, an exhibition at the Museum of Modern Art that explored that origins of one of the most problematic and to this day deeply misunderstood, and I think, dangerous, cultural practices—abstract painting.

The goal of abstract painting is simple but radical. Free a picture from the need to represent the world—real or imagined—and use line, color, and form alone to produce an emotion or feeling. These artists rendered their work even more useless and marginal than other paintings by refusing to represent the things of this world with which we already have relationships, such as persons, bouquets, and landscapes. The abstract painter and sculptor desired to create a powerful aesthetic experience *without* those extra artistic relationships. As the critic Roger Fry wrote, "They do not seek to imitate form, but to create form; not to imitate life, but to find an equivalent for life. . . . In fact, they aim not at illusion but at reality."[31]

But these artists experienced resistance from the public, the media, and their governments. Artists like Malevich felt obliged to defend themselves, to strengthen their absurd paintings through words. The exhibition's curator, Leah Dickerman, writes, "Faced with the fear that abstract work might be seen as simply arbitrary, its proponents compensated with words."[32] So they wrote about purity and directness of experience. But their writings, which theorized, pontificated, and thundered about transformation and a new world, testified against their fragile pictures and simply affirmed their

31. Quoted in Dickerman et al., eds., *Inventing Abstraction 1910–1925*, 28.
32. Ibid., 32.

absurdity. Their linguistic resistance, in the form of artist statements and manifestoes, created even *stronger* resistance.

It is not surprising that these pictures became targets and the artists who painted them were considered dangerous by governments fearful of the freedom to do absurdly wonderful things like paint pictures that had no real use—even though the artists and their supportive critics claimed for them all kinds of important uses, even talking about how these canvases could *transform society.*

Alfred H. Barr Jr. and MoMA

Although it is a celebration of the artists who risked a lot more than their careers to explore the implications of art forms that did something other than represent the empirical world, *Inventing Abstraction* also pays homage to an unlikely hero, a vulnerable and frail man, a rather uptight art historian, the son and grandson of Presbyterian ministers and Princeton Theological Seminary graduates, who, in his own way, just might have been responsible for saving many of these contradictions in paint, and even the persons who painted them.[33]

In 1933, Alfred H. Barr Jr., after four years on the job as founding director of the Museum of Modern Art, was granted a year's leave of absence due to nervous exhaustion. Barr and his wife spent the year in Germany, and he was horrified by what he saw. Hitler had been named chancellor that year, and the Nazi party had begun targeting abstract paintings (and their makers) as degenerates.

Barr was not concerned with the artist's writings, their ideas and theories and other forms of verbal justification. He worried about the paintings and the fate of their makers, many of whom were already in hiding or making plans to flee Germany and whose works had already been confiscated or locked away in storage.

And so this somewhat pedantic and nervous scholar embarked on a courageous course of action, a course of action reminiscent of Indiana Jones. He began to find ways to save the artists and their art by bringing them to New York. In addition to buying work directly from the artists and dealers, he conceived of an exhibition shortly after his return that would serve as cover for his rescue mission. Through the exhibition he was able to arrange for loans, which he planned to turn into purchases. Through his efforts and

---

33. For more information on Barr, see Kantor, *Alfred H. Barr, Jr. and the Intellectual Origins of the Museum of Modern Art* and Sandler, ed., *Defining Modern Art.*

the institutional protection provided by MoMA, New York City became safe for abstract painting and the embattled artists who painted them.

Barr's groundbreaking exhibition, entitled *Cubism and Abstract Art*, opened at the Museum of Modern Art in 1936, just one year before Hitler's notorious *Degenerate Art* exhibition. The exhibition was Barr's protest against fascism and a celebration of the human freedom embodied in those lines, colors, and forms. In the exhibition catalogue's introduction Barr writes:

> This essay and exhibition might well be dedicated to those painters of squares and circles (and the architects influenced by them) who have suffered at the hands of philistines with political power.[34]

Inventing Abstraction bears witness to the reality that artists, like Malevich, had hoped that their artistic artifacts would change the world and transform humanity. The artists were right to believe that their work was subversive. But in the end, they needed protection from the very people they hoped would be changed by them.

What is the contradiction of abstraction to which *Inventing Abstraction* bears witness?

The exhibition's curator, Leah Dickinson, can offer the answer.

> Abstraction's pioneers announced its arrival with great fanfare, using the language of purgation, dissolution, and repudiation. But it only became fully institutionalized as a project of *rescue, retrieval, and preservation* [my emphasis].[35]

Mark Rothko, one of the most famous abstract painters in the United States, himself a Russian immigrant, was right. It is a risky business to send a painting out into the world.

Thank God for Malevich, who had the courage to send *White on White* out into the world, which, on a dreary winter day many years ago, taught me to see even the most difficult and empty paintings as full of humanity, suffering, and love.

And thank God for Alfred H. Barr Jr., who loved abstract painting enough to bring *White on White* and so many others to New York City for you and for me.

---

34. Quoted in Dickerman et al., eds., *Inventing Abstraction 1910–1925*, 366.
35. Ibid., 369.

WHO'S AFRAID OF MODERN ART?

KIRK VARNEDOE'S LAST SONG[36]

If you was hit by a truck and you were lying in the gutter dying and you had time to sing *one* song before you turn to dirt, one song that lets others and God know about how you felt about your time on this earth . . . that sums you up, you tell me that you would sing that song, about how you are filled with joy and that you're gonna shout it? Or would you sing something different . . . something real?

—SAM PHILLIPS TO JOHNNY CASH, *WALK THE LINE* (2005)

Pictures of Nothing: Abstract Art Since Pollock is Kirk Varnedoe's one song. Varnedoe was indeed hit by a truck, in slow motion, having been diagnosed with cancer in 1996. Nearly five years later, his cancer had spread, and so Varnedoe, Chief Curator and Director of the Department of Painting and Sculpture at New York's Museum of Modern Art since 1989, and recipient of the MacArthur Foundation "genius grant" in 1984, was forced to resign in favor of a faculty appointment at the Institute for Advanced Study at Princeton. That would allow him time to complete one last project: his contribution to the prestigious A. W. Mellon Lectures in the Fine Arts at the National Gallery of Art in Washington, D.C. According to his friend and collaborator Adam Gopnik, "He supposed these lectures to be his last and intended them to be his most important work, the capstone of his career. He poured his whole life into them."[37] Varnedoe delivered them from March 30 to May 11, 2003. Three months after his sixth and final lecture, he was dead at the age of fifty-seven. Three years later these lectures were published in book form. They are remarkably fresh and conversational—not only because Varnedoe did not have a chance to edit and revise them, but also because he gave these lectures, as he did every other lecture, entirely from memory.

Not only were these lectures his last song, they amounted to a confession of faith. Gopnik observes, "These lectures were his testament of faith— he ends the last one by the iteration of the words, 'I believe'—but since the faith was explicitly not dogmatic, the faith it demands from us in turn is one of, well, asking more questions."[38]

---

36. An earlier version of this essay appeared at *Books & Culture Corner* (2006), www.booksandculture.com/articles/webexclusives/2006/november/061127a.html.

37. Adam Gopnik, "Preface," in Varnedoe, *Pictures of Nothing*, ix.

38. Ibid., xvi.

Abstraction

Varnedoe's topic was abstract art. While angering the vast majority of those who care little about art and confusing those who claim to care some about art, abstract art continues to vex even the specialists. Varnedoe's title is a pejorative phrase that he ironically appropriated from the notoriously sharp-tongued critic William Hazlitt, who described some of British painter J. M. W. Turner's misty, quasi-abstract landscapes of the 1840s as "pictures of nothing." By contrast, Varnedoe's lectures reveal the positive role of abstract art in modern cultural life. Varnedoe also intended his lectures to be a response to E. H. Gombrich's well-known Mellon Lectures of 1956, "Art and Illusion," which made a case for illusionism in art in response to the hegemony of abstraction at mid-century.[39]

Where Christian and secular prophets of artistic and cultural doom see nihilism and decay, Varnedoe sees infinite variety and creativity. "Abstract art," he writes, "while seeming insistently to reject and destroy representation, in fact steadily expands its possibilities." He continues, "Abstract art is a remarkable system of productions and destructions that expands our potential for expression and communication."[40]

Abstract art invites us to perceive finer and finer distinctions of line, form, color, and, most importantly, intention: "the less there is to look at, the more important it is that we look at it closely and carefully. This is critical [for] abstract art. Small differences make all the difference."[41] Popular wisdom considers abstract art an excuse for "tenured radicals" to disguise bad art in the cloak of theory, art that does not reflect skill in rendering likeness. On the contrary, Varnedoe insists, abstract art is difficult, it takes practice to understand, and if it is governed by rules that appear arbitrary, that only makes it like every other cultural practice.

But unlike many defenders of abstraction, Varnedoe was never burdened with academic theory. "Between the vague confusions of individual experience and the authority of big ideas," he said, "sign me up for experience first."[42] *Pictures of Nothing* is about looking closely at abstract art, something that very few culturally conservative critics, including Christian commentators, have done. Varnedoe takes very seriously Frank Stella's quip about his paintings, "What you see is what you see."

39. See Gombrich, *Art and Illusion*.
40. Varnedoe, *Pictures of Nothing*, 40.
41. Ibid., 8.
42. Ibid.

Varnedoe's lecture series starts with Jackson Pollock's drip paintings, then moves to Frank Stella's stripe paintings of the late fifties and the Minimalists Donald Judd, Robert Morris, and Carl Andre. He then looks at work influenced by the aesthetic vocabulary of Minimalism, such as Eva Hess's organic constructions, the site-specific work of Michael Heizer and Robert Smithson, and the early Richard Serra. Far from seeing it as the product of theory, Varnedoe shows how Minimalism exemplifies an "I've got to kick this to believe it empiricism."[43] Exploring satire and irony in abstraction, which typically plays off resemblances between abstract art and representational art, Varnedoe discusses the work of Robert Rauschenberg, Jasper Johns, Andy Warhol, Gerhardt Richter, and Cy Twombly. He concludes with a look at contemporary abstraction: Brice Marden, Robert Ryman, and Richard Serra's recent work.

Credo

Infused with the urgency of imminent death, these lectures are a public confession of what Varnedoe believed to be one of the most important locations of creativity and human presence in modern culture. *Pictures of Nothing* is nothing if not a celebration of nuances, those small differences that become expressive, that reveal themselves to those who gaze intently and with empathy. The humanity of abstract art is often found not in *what* it depicts but in *how* it is made and how the artifact forces us as viewers to attend to details we might not otherwise consider, details that are the products of intentional decisions. The human presence embodied in the slightest of adjustments of line, form, and color reveals that art is first and foremost an object *made* by a human being, and that this *making* entails finer and finer distinctions, distinctions that another human being experiences.

Indeed, Varnedoe's lectures suggest that to experience a Jackson Pollock drip painting or a Richard Serra steel piece one has to actually see it in person, to experience its real presence, that space that opens up between the artifact and the viewer. Authentic art does not merely rely on our knowledge—it adds to it through experience. This is as true of abstract art as it is of representational or, as Gombrich called it, "illusionistic" art.

In her acknowledgments, Varnedoe's wife, artist Elyn Zimmerman, observed:

> Kirk had the impossibly poignant task of distilling everything into what he knew would be his last public appearance. . . . In the

43. Ibid., 11.

last two years of his life he was sometimes overcome by frustration and despair, but Kirk was a player, and he was courageous. He gave us all he could in the time left to him, and for that I want to thank Kirk.[44]

Although his life was cut short, Varnedoe was given the gift of being able to sing one last song, the gift of being able to sum up all that he was about.

Last Words

Varnedoe concludes his Mellon Lectures, ending his last public appearance, with these words:

> In this, I have faith. In surprise, I guess is the word. I have faith, because of works of art like this. I believe in abstract art. If I have not been able to justify it, I can perhaps say with the pragmatist, with the literalist: There it is. I have shown it to you. It has been done. It is being done. And because it can be done, it will be done. And now; I am done.[45]

Requiescat in pace, Dr. Varnedoe.

HAYSTACKS AND SHADOWS

Time destroys all that it creates.

—ALDOUS HUXLEY

One of the most enjoyable aspects of teaching art history to college students is presenting to them an artist or work of art with which they have been long familiar, perhaps Michelangelo and his famous *Pietà* or Marcel Duchamp and his notorious *Fountain*, and opening it up to reveal something they had not noticed, taking it out of their familiar categories and re-enchanting it.

We love Claude Monet's paintings: charming scenes of nineteenth-century Parisian life, sun-drenched depictions of picnics, regattas, weekend walks, sunsets and sunrises, and those adorable haystacks. We enjoy the messy and bright-colored brushstrokes that suddenly come together in a delightful image. Reproductions of these paintings adorn greeting cards,

44. Ibid., 276.
45. Ibid., 272.

decorate walls of waiting rooms, and fill college dorm rooms. And thousands flock to museums to see the paintings themselves. This was not the case in Monet's day. Critics derided him as an "impressionist" who had the gall to exhibit his barely legible paint-smeared sketches as finished paintings. One critic even claimed that these paintings looked like Monet simply threw paint on the canvas.

Monet revolutionized landscape painting by killing it. Its traditional function was to serve as a backdrop for historical and religious narratives. The artist would travel to Italy and fill a notebook with drawings of trees, hills, and other geographical features, which he would spend the rest of his career incorporating into his landscape paintings. With their "italianated" flora and fauna, these paintings evoked a timeless golden age. Monet, on the other hand, took his easel out into the Parisian countryside and painted what he saw.

Rather than serving as stage sets for heroic narratives from classical literature or the Bible, Monet's landscapes celebrated the everyday experience of nineteenth-century bourgeois Parisian life. He was excoriated by critics and his fellow artists because his subjects were not worthy of art, the goal of which was to represent the timeless essence of the Good, the True, and the Beautiful. A painting was supposed to stand outside of time. Thus in classical painting the sun always shone at high noon, which, by minimizing shadows, provided the most "rational" and "timeless" expression of virtue in paint.

In contrast, when Monet left the controlled environs of his studio and dragged his canvases and paints into the countryside, he went to battle with the shadows, with the temporal, the ephemeral, transitory, and local. Monet, not Kinkade, is the painter of light—a light that always fades. Whether presenting a bouquet of flowers, a couple enjoying a picnic, or a haystack, Monet was concerned with depicting his subject as constituted by light—but that light was ever changing.

Monet painted dozens and dozens of haystacks in 1891. He was fascinated by their change in appearance at different times of the day and at different times throughout the year. These charming paintings of a rural French countryside are in fact knock-down, drag-out, bare-knuckle fistfights with light. And they are battles that Monet always lost. To paint the play of light on haystacks in the morning or at dusk is to paint a subject that never stands still. Every painting of the haystacks is a painting of a subject that disappeared right before his eyes. The quick brushstrokes that we see on these canvases is evidence of Monet's urgency, his desperation to beat the clock.

Each of these paintings, then, is a failure, for it is incapable ultimately of "capturing" or rendering its subject in its essence. Painting can only offer a glimpse, a fragment, a part of the haystack as it emerges and ultimately disappears through time. Rather than depict triumphantly the Good, the True, and the Beautiful, Monet's humble haystacks (like all of his canvases) confess their own weakness, failure, and inability to grasp the magic of the natural world, the glow of our experiences of the world, which are always tempered by our realization that this moment will never return. Monet's intention was to exhibit all of his haystack paintings together, as a single expression of his failure to capture the haystack, to freeze time. For perhaps the first time in the Western tradition, painting was defined by what it could not do, was defined by its failure.

To stand in front of a painting by Monet is to be reminded of what Job confessed, "The Lord gave and the Lord has taken away" (Job 1:21). And yet, even through death, loss, and brokenness the world still crackles with the electricity of wonder and astonishment. And in spite of the impossibility and futility of Monet's task, of the task of art in general, it is worth it, even if it is only a glimpse.

And so it seems that even in their weakness and failure—in the limp that these paintings bear after their struggle with light and time—they nevertheless endure, persist, and persevere. They even seem to whisper defiantly in our ear, "This is not the end." For although that day has passed, as has that haystack as well as the man who painted it, somehow, miraculously, the painting remains, a message in a bottle, painted for us, for the future.

These paintings of haystacks (and perhaps all great painting) bear witness to the hope that if all is passing away, perhaps brokenness and death might as well.

THE CREATURELY PAINTING OF PAUL CÉZANNE

Modern art remains a mystery to most of us, and the paintings of Paul Cézanne might be the most perplexing of all. Neither fish nor fowl, they seem to hover somewhere between failed representation and almost—but not quite—abstraction.

And yet, as Alex Danchev's biography *Cézanne: A Life* reveals, these strange canvases had a tremendous impact on artists during his lifetime and have continued to fascinate artists, writers, and philosophers into the present. Henri Matisse, who in 1899 made a significant financial sacrifice to acquire *Three Bathers*, said that "it has sustained me morally in the critical moments of my venture as an artist . . . I have drawn from it my faith and my perseverance."[46]

Cézanne was adamant that painting is an ethical act, requiring a moral attitude. "You have to be incorruptible in your art," he claimed, "and to be so in your art, you have to train yourself to be so in your life."[47] What are we to make of such claims for these wobbly paintings, sloping still lifes, clunky landscapes, awkward figures?

Cézanne's artistic project was simple: paint nature. It is hard to exaggerate just how radical this is. The entire modern project was driven by a recommitment to nature. When artists began to open their eyes, go out into nature and paint *sur le motif*, as Cézanne called it, nature became strange and mysterious. Cézanne admitted, "Nature appears to me so complicated."[48] Every painting for him was a struggle to understand the object before him.

In contrast, the artistic establishment pillaged nature in order to perfect it, using it as a backdrop for classical and biblical stories that shaped virtue or delighted the soul. Not so for Cézanne. "You don't paint souls, you paint bodies; and when the bodies are well-painted, dammit, the soul—if they have one—the soul shines through all over the place."[49]

A distinctive feature of Cézanne's paintings is their heft. He seems to gauge the weight of every subject, whether an apple, an oak tree, or a chunk of the Mediterranean Sea. And Cézanne himself said, "I paint a head like a door, like anything else."[50] This kind of "anarchistic painting," as Danchev calls it, in which every element in a composition is treated in the same manner, has been threatening to art critics, theologians, and the general public, who discern in such rigorous and egalitarian materiality and physicality a denial of the preeminence of the human being that distinguishes him or her from the rest of the nature. Cézanne's pictures often offend our inner theologians of glory, who want to see our own distorted images of self-importance reflected back to us.

Cézanne's approach to painting does not entertain our vanity. One of the more important insights of the Reformation was to restore the dignity of the human being *as a creature* and the world as a gift. If Athanasius claimed that God became man so that man could become God, Luther argued that God became man so that man could once again become a creature, could take delight in his created, contingent, creaturely nature—become a happy

---

46. Quoted in Danchev, *Cézanne*, 15.

47. Quoted in ibid., 27.

48. Quoted in ibid., 258.

49. Quoted in ibid., 103.

50. Quoted in ibid., 296.

human rather than a grumpy god. As Oswald Bayer writes, through Christ "we enter into a new worldliness."[51]

Perhaps this is Cézanne's singular achievement. He returned painting to the realm of the creation. These paintings are worldly, creaturely. The critics noticed this. One hostile writer claimed that Cézanne could even paint bad breath. Yet Luther himself claimed that God is "in the manure bug or even in the cesspool . . . no less than in heaven."[52] Too often art is regarded as a means to climb the ladder of divine ascent, to aspire to the heavens and commune with the divine. For Cézanne art is a creaturely practice, one that revels in nature. He exclaimed, "Oh, nature, nature! Who has ever plumbed its secrets?"[53] After his death, Cézanne's friend Ravaisou observed, "He loved nature with a passion, perhaps to the exclusion of all else; he painted in order to prolong within himself the joy of living among the trees."[54] And another added, "he had no real friends except trees."[55] Cézanne himself confessed about a particular tree, "It's a living being . . . I love it like an old friend. It knows everything about my life and gives me excellent advice. I should like to be buried at its feet."[56] Cézanne most definitely follows the Psalmist's avowal that nature "speaks" (Ps 19:1–2).

Therefore, unlike Edvard Munch, who seemed to be terrorized by it, Cézanne was mesmerized by nature, fascinated by it riches, and thoroughly at home with it. For him his work as an artist was entirely devoted to serving it. But what is important to note is that it is not nature, bereft of God, that Cézanne experienced, but nature as a gift from God. "To see the work of God, that's what I apply myself to."[57] Heidegger claims that Cézanne's paintings assert that "life is terrifying," but these paintings see something more, as do their maker, who believed that the world that so captivated him was God's. Oswald Bayer notes that "creation"—nature (and culture)as a gift of God—is in fact a confession of faith and not self-evident. It is the work of faith that transforms brute, crushing nature that is terrifying into a gift from God to be received, experienced, "heard" as a promise of love.[58]

Perhaps Matisse was right after all: there is something in Cézanne's paintings in which to trust.

51. Bayer, *Living by Faith*, 28.

52. Quoted in Bayer, *Martin Luther's Theology*, 105.

53. Quoted in Danchev, *Cézanne*, 259.

54. Quoted in ibid., 329.

55. Quoted in ibid., 328.

56. Quoted in ibid., 330.

57. Quoted in ibid., 293.

58. Bayer, *Martin Luther's Theology*, 95–105.

Afterword

Cézanne observed, "The main thing in a painting is finding the right distance."[59] This distance is the space within a painting—the distance between objects in the painting as well as the distance between the eye of the painter and the canvas itself. It has been observed that Cézanne painted from two distances—nose to nose and about ten feet. But the "right distance" is also that between the painting and the viewer. Walter Benjamin noticed *this* distance:

> As I was looking at an extraordinarily beautiful Cézanne, it suddenly occurred to me that to the extent that one grasps a painting, one does not in any way enter into its space; rather, this space thrusts itself forward, especially in various specific spots.[60]

The distance that a painting creates initiates a relationship with the viewer. It creates, actualizes, makes present a complex relationship between the world, the viewer, and God—even if "God" is experienced as hidden or absent, as an echo, a haunting presence of judgment, guilt, or fear. To experience a painting is to be addressed by it, to be responsive to what says, and, following Rilke, to be claimed by it ("you must change your life!"). This distance is theological. As Rowan Williams has written,

> To be absorbed in the sheer otherness of any created order or beauty is to open the door to God, because it involves that basic displacement of the dominating ego without which there can be no spiritual growth.[61]

A painting offers this "sheer otherness" to the viewer—an otherness, however, that "speaks," that addresses us, because it is the aesthetic result of an artist coming to grips with the world, himself, and God through paint on canvas.

How will *you* respond?

59. Quoted in Danchev, *Cézanne*, 305.
60. Quoted in ibid., 365.
61. Williams, *The Wound of Knowledge*, 188.

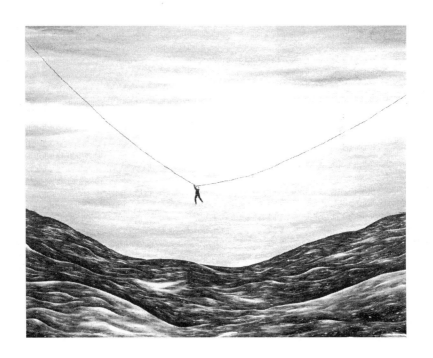

BIBLIOGRAPHY

Auden, W. H. "Today's wonder-world needs Alice" (1962). In *Forewords and Afterwords*, 283–93. New York: Vintage, 1990.

Ballor, Jordon. *Get Your Hands Dirty: Essays on Christian Social Thought*. Eugene, OR: Wipf & Stock, 2013.

Bastian, Heiner, ed. *Andy Warhol: Retrospective*. Los Angeles: MoCA/Tate, 2001.

Bayer, Oswald. *A Contemporary in Dissent: Johann Georg Hamann as a Radical Enlightener*. Grand Rapids: Eerdmans, 2012.

———. "The Ethics of Gift." *Lutheran Quarterly* 24 (2010) 447–68.

———. *Freedom in Response: Lutheran Ethics: Sources and Controversies*. New York: Oxford University Press, 2007.

———. *Living by Faith: Justification and Sanctification*. Grand Rapids: Eerdmans, 2003.

———. *Martin Luther's Theology: A Contemporary Interpretation*. Grand Rapids: Eerdmans, 2008.

———. "The Modern Narcissus." *Lutheran Quarterly* 9/3 (1995) 301–13.

———. *Theology the Lutheran Way*. Grand Rapids: Eerdmans, 2007.

Betz, John R. *After Enlightenment: The Post-Secular Vision of J. G. Hamann*. London: Blackwell, 2012.

Bloom, Harold. *A Map of Misreading*. London: Oxford University Press, 1975.

Boucher, Brian. "Andres Serrano *Piss Christ* Still Pissing Off Christians." *Art in America*, September 25, 2012. www.artinamerica.magazine.com/news-features/news/piss-christ.

Brodsky, Joseph. *Less Than One*. New York: Farrar, Straus & Giroux, 1986.

Buechner, Frederick. *Telling the Truth: The Gospel as Tragedy, Comedy, and Fairy Tale*. New York: HarperOne, 1977.

Bunge, Gabriel. *The Rublev Trinity: The Icon of the Trinity by the Monk-Painter Andrei Rublev*. Crestwood, NY: St. Vladimir's Seminary Press, 2007.

Courbet, Gustave. "Art Cannot Be Taught." In *Realism and Tradition in Art 1848–1900*, edited by Linda Nochlin, 34–36. Englewood Cliffs, NJ: Prentice Hall, 1966.

Danchev, Alex. *Cézanne: A Life*. New York: Pantheon, 2012.

Danchev, Alex, ed. and trans. *The Letters of Paul Cézanne*. Los Angeles: Getty, 2013.

Danto, Arthur. "The Artworld." *Journal of Philosophy* 61/19 (October 5, 1964) 571–84.

Dickie, George. *Art and the Aesthetic*. Ithaca, NY: Cornell University Press, 1974.

———. *The Art Circle: A Theory of Art*. New York: Haven, 1984.

Dickerman, Leah, et al., eds. *Inventing Abstraction 1910–1925: How a Radical Idea Changed Modern Art*. New York: Thames & Hudson, 2013.

Dostoyevsky, Fyodor. *The Brothers Karamazov*. London: Penguin, 1993.

Dutton, Denis. *The Art Instinct: Beauty, Pleasure, and Human Evolution*. Bloomsbury, 2010.

Duvignaud, Jean. *The Sociology of Art*. New York: Harper & Row, 1972.

Ebeling, Gerhard. *Luther: An Introduction to His Thought*. Minneapolis: Fortress, 2007.

————. *Word and Faith*. London: SCM, 1963.

Egbert, Donald Drew. "The Idea of 'Avant-Garde' in Art and Politics." *The American Historical Review* 73/2 (December 1967) 339–66.

Eliot, T. S. *To Criticize the Critic*. New York: Octagon, 1980.

————. "Tradition and the Individual Talent" (1917). In *Selected Essays: 1917–1932*, 3–11. New York: Harcourt, Brace & Co., 1932.

Foucault, Michel. *The Order of Things*. New York: Pantheon, 1971.

Forde, Gerhard. *On Being a Theologian of the Cross: Reflections on Luther's Heidelberg Disputation 1518*. Grand Rapids: Eerdmans, 1997.

Fried, Michael. *Manet's Modernism or the Face of Painting in the 1860s*. Chicago: University of Chicago Press, 1998.

Fuller, Randall. "The Image of a Writer." *Humanities* 33/6 (November-December 2012). www.neh.gov/humanities/2012/novemberdecember/features/the-image-writer.

Gianvito, John, ed. *Andrei Tarkovsky Interviews*. Oxford, MS: University Press of Mississippi, 2006.

Gombrich, Ernst H. *Art and Illusion: A Study in the Psychology of Pictorial Representation*. Princeton, NJ: Princeton University Press, 2000.

Gould, Steven Jay. "Evolution: The Pleasures of Pluralism." *New York Review of Books*, June 26, 1997. www.nybooks.com/articles/archives/1997/jun/26/evolution-the-pleasures-of-pluralism/.

Hudgins, Andrew. "Piss Christ." www.slate.com/articles/arts/poem/2000/04/piss_christ.html.

Hughes, Robert. *American Visions: The Epic History of Art in America*. New York: Knopf, 1997.

Hugo, Victor. *Les Misérables*. New York: Signet Classics, 1987.

Hunter, James Davison. *Culture Wars: The Struggle to Control the Family, Art, Education, Law, and Politics in America*. New York: Basic, 1992.

————. *To Change the World: The Irony, Tragedy, and Possibility of Christianity in the Late Modern World*. London: Oxford University Press, 2010.

Huxley, Aldous. *Huxley and God: Essays*. New York: Harper, 1992.

Iwand, Hans J. *The Righteousness of Faith According to Luther*. Eugene, OR: Wipf and Stock, 2008.

Kantor, Sybil Gordon. *Alfred H. Barr, Jr. and the Intellectual Origins of the Museum of Modern Art*. Cambridge, MA: MIT Press, 2002.

Keller, Tim, and Katherine Leary Alsdorf. *Every Good Endeavor: Connecting Your Work to God's Work*. New York: Norton, 2012.

Kerr, Fergus. *Theology After Wittgenstein*. Oxford: Basil Blackwell, 1986.

Koerner, Joseph Leo. *The Moment of Self-Portraiture in German Renaissance Art*. Chicago: University of Chicago Press, 1993.

Krauss, Rosalind. "A View of Modernism." *Artforum* 11/1 (September 1972) 48–51.

Kuspit, Donald B. *The Critic is Artist: The Intentionality of Art*. Ann Arbor, MI: UMI Research Press, 1984.

————. "Forum: Art Students" (1984). In *Redeeming Art: Critical Reveries*, 7–10. New York: Visual Arts/Allworth Press, 2000.

Kuyper, Abraham. *Lectures on Calvinism*. Grand Rapids: Eerdmans, 1931.

Luther, Martin. *On Christian Liberty*. Minneapolis: Augsburg Fortress, 2003.

————. "Definition of Faith." In *An Introduction to St. Paul's Letter to the Romans.* Translated by R. Smith. http://www.iclnet.or/pub/resources/text/wittenberg/luther/luther-faith.txt.

————. "The Disputation Concerning Man" (1536). In *Luther's Works*, vol. 34, translated by L. Spitz, J. Pelikan, H. Oswald, and H. Zehmann, 133–44. Minneapolis: Fortress, 1999.

Mandelstam, Osip. "On the Addressee." In *Critical Prose and Letters*, 67–73. New York: Ardis, 1979.

Martínez Celaya, Enrique. "On Painting." In *Collected Writings*, 240–47. Lincoln, NE: University of Nebraska Press, 2011.

McGrath, Charles. "Good Art, Bad People." *New York Times,* June 21, 2012. www.nytimes.com/2012/06/22/opinion/global-agenda-magazine-good-art-bad-people.html.

Melville, Herman. *Moby-Dick; or, The Whale*. New York: Norton, 2002.

Mouw, Richard. *When the Kings Come Marching In: Isaiah and the New Jerusalem.* Grand Rapids: Eerdmans, 2002.

Niederkorn, William. "The Man Behind A Controversy Andres Serrano . . ." *The Inquirer*, August 26, 1989. Articles.philly.com/1989-08-26/news/26148343_1_Jesus-pictures-works.

Nietzsche, Friedrich. "Thus Spoke Zarathustra." In *The Portable Nietzsche,* 121–439. New York: Penguin, 1982.

Nochlin, Linda, ed. *Realism and Tradition in Art 1848–1900*. Englewood Cliffs, NJ: Prentice Hall, 1966.

Ortega y Gasset, José. *The Dehumanization of Art: And Other Essays on Art, Culture, and Literature*. Princeton, NJ: Princeton University Press, 1968.

————. "Introduction." In *Six Color Reproductions by Diego Velázquez in the Prado Museum*, 6–18. Oxford: Oxford University Press, 1946.

————. "Velázquez and His Fame." In *Velázquez*, 10–18. New York: Random House, 1953.

Pascal, Blaise. *Pensées*. Edited and translated by Roger Arlew. Indianapolis: Hackett, 2005.

Pelikan, Jaroslav. *The Vindication of Tradition*. New Haven, CT: Yale University Press, 1984.

Pinker, Steven. *How the Mind Works*. New York: Norton, 1997.

"Portrait of the artist as an entrepreneur." *The Economist*, December 17, 2011. www.economist.com/node/21541710

Potok, Chaim. *My Name is Asher Lev*. New York: Random House, 1972.

Prelinger, Elizabeth. *After the Scream: The Late Paintings of Edvard Munch*. New Haven, CT: Yale University Press, 2002.

Prideaux, Sue. *Edvard Munch: Behind the Scream*. New Haven, CT: Yale University Press, 2005.

Rice, Andrew. "Damien Hirst: Jumping the Shark." *Bloomberg Businessweek,* November 21, 2012. www.businessweek.com/articles/2012-11-21/damien-hirst-jumping-the-shark.

Rilke, Rainer Maria. *Letters on Cézanne.* Translated by J. Agee. New York: North Point, 2002.

Rosenberg, Harold. "The American Action Painters" (1952). In *The Tradition of the New,* 23–39. New York: Horizon, 1959.

Rousseau, Jean-Jacques. *Emile: or On Education.* Translated by Alan Bloom. New York: Basic, 1979.

Sandler, Irving, ed. *Defining Modern Art: Selected Writings of Alfred H. Barr, Jr.* New York: Abrams, 1986.

Scruton, Roger. *Culture Counts: Faith and Feeling in a World Besieged.* New York: Encounters, 2007.

Serraller, Francisco Caalvo, and Miguel Delibes. *Antonio López García: Paintings and Sculpture.* New York: DAP Publishers, 2001.

Sherman, Amy. *Kingdom Calling: Vocational Stewardship for the Common Good.* Downers Grove, IL: InterVarsity, 2011.

Siedell, Daniel A. "After the End: The Artistic Practice of Hope." In *The world has won. A final bow was taken,* 56–61. Des Moines: Des Moines Art Center, 2010.

———. *God in the Gallery: A Christian Embrace of Modern Art.* Grand Rapids: Baker Academic Press, 2008.

———. "Icons and Iconoclasm." *The City* (Spring 2010) 108–15.

———. "The Mark of Cain: Figure and Landscape in the Work of Enrique Martínez Celaya." *IMAGE* 70 (Summer 2011) 33–40.

Smith, Roberta. "Hirst, Globally Dotting His 'I.'" *The New York Times,* January 12, 2012. www.nytimes.com/2012/01/13/arts/design/damien-hirsts-spot-paintings-at-gagosian-in-eight-cities.html?_r=0.

Sontag, Susan. "Against Interpretation" (1964). In *Against Interpretation and Other Essays,* 3–14. New York: Octagon, 1986.

Steiner, George. *Real Presences.* Chicago: University of Chicago Press, 1991.

Tarkovsky, Andrei. *Sculpting in Time: Reflections on the Cinema.* Austin, TX: University of Texas Press, 1986.

Temkin, Ann. *Edvard Munch.* New York: MoMA, 2012.

Thompson, Don. *The $12 Million Stuffed Shark: The Curious Economics of Contemporary Art.* New York: Palgrave/Macmillan, 2008.

Thornton, Sarah. *Seven Days in the Art World.* New York: Norton, 2008.

———. "Sexy Contemporary Antiquities." *The Economist,* July 7, 2012. www.economist.com/node/21558235

Tinterow, Gary, ed. *Manet/Velázquez: The French Taste for Spanish Painting.* New York: Metropolitan Museum of Art, 2003.

Tøjner, Paul Erik. *Munch in His Own Words.* Munich: Prestel, 2003.

Varnedoe, Kirk. *Pictures of Nothing: Abstract Art Since Pollock.* Princeton, NJ: Princeton University Press, 2006.

Varnedoe, Kirk, Pepe Karmel, et al. *Jackson Pollock.* New York: MoMA, 1998.

Veith, Gene. *God at Work: Your Christian Vocation in All of Life.* Wheaton, IL: Crossway, 2011.

Vogel, Carol. "Damien Hirst's Next Sensation—Thinking Outside the Dealer." *The New York Times,* September 14, 2008. www.nytimes.com/2008/09/15/arts/design/15avct.html?pagewanted=all

Wallace, David Foster. *This is Water.* Boston: Little Brown, 2009.

Wilde, Oscar. "The Critic As Artist." In *De Profundis, The Ballad of Reading Gaol & Other Writings,* 175–243. London: Wordsworth Classics, 1999.

Williams, Rowan. *The Wound of Knowledge: Christian Spirituality from the New Testament to St. John of the Cross.* Cambridge, MA: Cowley, 1990.

Wiman, Christian. *My Bright Abyss: Meditations of a Modern Believer.* New York: Farrar, Strauss & Giroux, 2013.

Wolterstorff, Nicholas. *Art in Action: Towards a Christian Aesthetic.* Grand Rapids: Eerdmans, 1987.

Woolf, Virginia. "Lewis Carroll." In *The Moment and Other Essays,* vol. 1, edited by L. Woolf, 81–83. London, 1966.